25 Cozy Crocheted Slippers

Kristi Simpson

STACKPOLE BOOKS

Copyright © 2015 by Kristi Simpson
Published by
STACKPOLE BOOKS
5067 Ritter Road
Mechanicsburg, PA 17055
www.stackpolebooks.com

All rights reserved, including the right to reproduce this book or portions thereof in any form or by any means, electronic or mechanical, including recording or by any information storage and retrieval system, without permission in writing from the publisher. All inquiries should be addressed to Stackpole Books, 5067 Ritter Road, Mechanicsburg, PA 17055.

The contents of this book are for personal use only. Patterns contained herein may be reproduced in limited quantities for such use. Any large-scale commercial reproduction is prohibited without the written consent of the publisher.

Printed in the United States of America

10 9 8 7 6 5 4 3 2 1

First edition
Cover design by Caroline Stover
Photography by Kristi Simpson

Library of Congress Cataloging-in-Publication Data
Simpson, Kristi.
    25 cozy crocheted slippers : fun & fashionable footwear for the whole family / Kristi Simpson. — First edition.
        pages   cm
    ISBN 978-0-8117-1408-2
    1. Crocheting—Patterns. 2. Footwear. I. Title. II. Title: Twenty-five cozy crocheted slippers.
TT825.S54625 2015
746.43'4—dc23

2015017163

Contents

Acknowledgments	vi
Introduction	1
Shell-Edged Striped Slippers	2
Grace Sandals	5
Fun in the Sun Strappy Sandals	8
So Comfy Basketweave Socks	10
Fuzzy Scuffs	13
Rainbow Ruffle Slipper Boots	17
Just Peachy Slipper Socks	20
Dad Loafers	24
Pearls & Lace Little Princess Slippers	28
Sandy Button Sandals	31
Shaggy Boots	36
Men's Goldenrod Slipper Socks	39
Frog Loafers	42
Cabled Slipper Socks	45
Striped Mary Jane Slippers	48
Interlocking Rings Barefoot Sandals	51
Ruby Red Slippers	54
Fabulous Faux Cable Loafers	57
Owl Boots	61
Elfin Boot Slippers	65
Simply Divine Moccasins	68
Double-Strap Slip-Ons	70
Miss Kitty Slippers	73
Super Kozy Kidz Slipper Socks	76
Twilight Boots	78
How to Read My Patterns	81
Stitch Guide	83
Finishing Touches	101
Visual Index	104

Acknowledgments

I enjoyed photographing these shoes so much with my family and friends. I want to give a huge shout out to Photo Prop Floors & Backdrops for their incredible floordrops and backdrops. Their customer service and products are beyond professional. Also, I want to give thanks to Erin of Fancy Fabrics for her contribution to the book. I appreciate your donations and support.

Next, a big thank-you to my many testers for their time and effort. Also, I must give thanks to Pam Hoenig, my editor, for her hard work and to the rest of the Stackpole team for their assistance.

And last but not least, I need to give a million thanks to my sweet family. You put up with my crochet mess and craftiness, and you still love me . . . Jason, I love you so much. You make my dreams come true *and* then shower me with yarn! Thanks for being my biggest fan and pushing me daily to be the best I can be. Jacob, Kimberly, Allison, James, and Ryan, you're the best kiddos and you're more than I could ever ask for . . . I love you all to the moon and back . . . and then some!

Introduction

As a kid I wandered into my aunt's closet one evening and I remember seeing a sight I'll never forget! SHOES! They were everywhere—all sorts of colors and styles. I couldn't believe that one person could have so many different shoes! In particular, I remember a sparkly gold pair that just bedazzled me. I imagined that my aunt had a pair for every outfit or maybe even every day of the year!

Looking back, I'm sure there weren't as many as my memory recollects (or maybe there were!). Fortunately for you, I was inspired that night. At that time, it wasn't for crochet designs, but fast forward twenty-plus years, and voila!

I promise that you are going to love crocheting your own slippers! Why? One reason is that you can have the comfort you crave with the design you love. Also, the designs in this book are perfect for any season, no matter the temperature. Multiple sizes for each pattern give you the flexibility to make whatever pattern you choose for whomever you choose. Snuggle up with your hook and yarn and make your very own pair of slippers, socks, or loafers!

To ensure success, you *must* pay close attention to gauge. If you don't, you'll end up with clown shoes or Barbie slippers. You'll find designs at all levels of skill. If you've never crocheted slippers before, and even if you are an experienced crocheter, it's a good idea to start with an easy pattern just to get the feel of it, then move on to more challenging designs.

The memory of seeing all of those shoes in my aunt's closet has stuck with me for many years, and now through crochet I have been able to add my own designs for slippers and shoes to my closet. I hope you enjoy adding to your own collection of footwear!

These slippers, worked up in single and double crochet, are so stylish with their stripes and shell edging. You'll love them!

Finished Measurements
Women's Small: 8"/20.5 cm long, 3.5"/8.9 cm wide
Women's Medium: 9"/23 cm long, 4"/10 cm wide
Women's Large: 10"/25.5 cm long, 4"/10 cm wide

Yarn
- Caron Simply Soft, medium worsted weight #4 yarn, 100% acrylic (315 yd/288 m, 6 oz/170 g per skein)
  1 skein #9761 Plum Perfect (Color A)
  1 skein #9759 Ocean (Color B)
  1 skein #9702 Off White (Color C)

Hook and Other Materials
- US E-4/3.5 mm crochet hook or size to obtain gauge
- Stitch marker
- Yarn needle

Gauge
16 sts and 20 rows in sc = 4"/10 cm square

Notes
- The slipper is crocheted back to front in rows. It is then folded and sewn at the front and back. To finish, the shell edging is crocheted around the opening for the foot.
- To change colors, push the hook through the next stitch, pull the yarn back through, yarn over with the *next* color, and pull through. Color change is complete. For a tutorial, see page 99.
- For a tutorial on Single Crochet Decrease (sc dec), see page 87.

Small (make 2)
Using Color A, ch31.
Row 1: Turn, sc in second chain from hook and in each across (30 sts).
Rows 2–3: Turn, ch1, sc in each stitch.
Join Color B, fasten off Color A.
Rows 4–6: Turn, ch1, sc in each stitch (30 sts).
Join Color C, fasten off Color B.
Rows 7–9: Turn, ch1, sc in each stitch.
Join Color A, fasten off Color C.
Rows 10–12: Turn, ch1, sc in each stitch.
Join Color B, fasten off Color A.
Rows 13–15: Turn, ch1, sc in each stitch.
Join Color C, fasten off Color B.
Rows 16–18: Turn, ch1, sc in each stitch.
Join Color A, fasten off Color C.
Rows 19–27: Turn, ch1, sc in each stitch.
Row 28: Mark beginning of row with stitch marker. Turn, ch1, sc dec, sc26, sc dec (28 sts).
Row 29: Turn, ch1, sc in each stitch.
Row 30: Turn, ch1, sc dec, sc24, sc dec (26 sts).
Row 31: Turn, ch1, sc in each stitch.
Row 32: Turn, ch1, sc dec, sc22, sc dec (24 sts).
Row 33: Turn, ch1, sc in each stitch.
Row 34: Turn, ch1, sc dec, sc20, sc dec (22 sts).
Row 35: Turn, ch1, sc in each stitch.
Row 36: Turn, ch1, sc dec, sc18, sc dec (20 sts).
Row 37: Turn, ch1, sc in each stitch.
Row 38: Turn, sc dec, sc16, sc dec (18 sts).
Row 39: Turn, sc in each stitch.
Row 40: Turn, sc dec, sc14, sc dec (16 sts).
Fasten off. Weave in ends.
Using yarn needle and the appropriate color yarn for each stripe, sew top of slipper together from Row 40 to Row 28 at stitch marker. The seam will be on the top of the slipper.
Sew toe end closed so that it lies flat.
Fold the beginning and end of Row 1 together and sew a seam to create the heel.
Fasten off. Weave in all ends.

Medium (make 2)
Using Color A, ch31.
Row 1: Turn, sc in second chain from hook and in each across (30 sts).
Rows 2–3: Turn, ch1, sc in each stitch.
Join Color B, fasten off Color A.
Rows 4–6: Turn, ch1, sc in each stitch.
Join Color C, fasten off Color B.
Rows 7–9: Turn, ch1, sc in each stitch.
Join Color A, fasten off Color C.
Rows 10–12: Turn, ch1, sc in each stitch.
Join Color B, fasten off Color A.
Rows 13–15: Turn, ch1, sc in each stitch.
Join Color C, fasten off Color B.
Rows 16–18: Turn, ch1, sc in each stitch.
Join Color A, fasten off Color C.
Rows 19–21: Turn, ch1, sc in each stitch.

Join Color B, fasten off Color A.
Rows 22–24: Turn, ch1, sc in each stitch.
Join Color C, fasten off Color B.
Rows 25–27: Turn, ch1, sc in each stitch.
Join Color A, fasten off Color C.
Rows 28–30: Mark beginning of Row 28 with a stitch marker. Turn, ch1, sc in each stitch.
Rows 31–32: Turn, ch1, sc in each stitch.
Row 33: Turn, ch1, sc dec, sc26, sc dec (28 sts).
Row 34: Turn, ch1, sc in each stitch.
Row 35: Turn, ch1, sc dec, sc24, sc dec (26 sts).
Row 36: Turn, ch1, sc in each stitch.
Row 37: Turn, ch1, sc dec, sc22, sc dec (24 sts).
Row 38: Turn, ch1, sc in each stitch.
Row 39: Turn, ch1, sc dec, sc20, sc dec (22 sts).
Row 40: Turn, ch1, sc in each stitch.
Row 41: Turn, ch1, sc dec, sc18, sc dec (20 sts).
Row 42: Turn, ch1, sc in each stitch.
Row 43: Turn, sc dec, sc16, sc dec (18 sts).
Row 44: Turn, sc in each stitch.
Row 45: Turn, sc dec, sc14, sc dec (16 sts).
Fasten off. Weave in ends.
Using yarn needle and appropriate color yarn for each stripe, sew top of slipper together from Row 45 to Row 28 at stitch marker. The seam will be on the top of the slipper. Next, sew toe end closed so that it lies flat.
Fold the beginning and end of Row 1 together and sew a seam to create the heel.
Fasten off. Weave in all ends.

Large (make 2)

Using Color A, ch31.
Row 1: Turn, sc in second chain from hook and in each across (30 sts).
Rows 2–3: Turn, ch1, sc in each stitch.
Join Color B, fasten off Color A.
Rows 4–6: Turn, ch1, sc in each stitch.
Join Color C, fasten off Color B.
Rows 7–9: Turn, ch1, sc in each stitch.
Join Color A, fasten off Color C.
Rows 10–12: Turn, ch1, sc in each stitch.
Join Color B, fasten off Color A.
Rows 13–15: Turn, ch1, sc in each stitch.
Join Color C, fasten off Color B.
Rows 16–18: Turn, ch1, sc in each stitch.
Join Color A, fasten off Color C.
Rows 19–21: Turn, ch1, sc in each stitch.
Join Color B, fasten off Color A.
Rows 22–24: Turn, ch1, sc in each stitch.
Join Color C, fasten off Color B.
Rows 25–27: Turn, ch1, sc in each stitch.
Join Color A, fasten off Color C.
Rows 28–30: Mark Row 28 with a stitch marker. Turn, ch1, sc in each stitch.
Join Color B, fasten off Color A.
Rows 31–33: Turn, ch1, sc in each stitch.
Join Color C, fasten off Color B.
Rows 34–36: Turn, ch1, sc in each stitch.
Join Color A, fasten off Color B.
Rows 36–37: Turn, ch1, sc in each stitch.
Row 38: Turn, ch1, sc dec, sc26, sc dec (28 sts).
Row 39: Turn, ch1, sc in each stitch.
Row 40: Turn, ch1, sc dec, sc24, sc dec (26 sts).
Row 41: Turn, ch1, sc in each stitch.
Row 42: Turn, ch1, sc dec, sc22, sc dec (24 sts).
Row 43: Turn, ch1, sc in each stitch.
Row 44: Turn, ch1, sc dec, sc20, sc dec (22 sts).
Row 45: Turn, ch1, sc in each stitch.
Row 46: Turn, ch1, sc dec, sc18, sc dec (20 sts).
Row 47: Turn, ch1, sc in each stitch.
Row 48: Turn, sc dec, sc16, sc dec (18 sts).
Row 49: Turn, sc in each stitch.
Row 50: Turn, sc dec, sc14, sc dec (16 sts).
Fasten off. Weave in all ends.
Using yarn needle and the appropriate color yarn for each stripe, sew top of slipper together from Row 50 to Row 28 at stitch marker. The seam will be on the top of the slipper.
Sew toe end closed so that it lies flat.
Fold the beginning and end of Row 1 together and sew a seam to create the heel.
Fasten off. Weave in all ends.

Edging for All Sizes

Rnd 1: Join Color A at seam on Row 1, ch2 (does not count as a stitch), using ends of rows as stitches, dc27 down along one side of opening of slipper, dc in front center, dc27 along other side of opening, sl st to first stitch to join.
Rnd 2: Ch1, *skip 2 stitches, 5dc stitches in next stitch, skip 2 stitches, sl st in next stitch, repeat from * 3 more times, ch5, skip 5 stitches (this will be the front center), sl st to next stitch, **skip 2 stitches, 5dc in next stitch, skip 2 stitches, sl st in next, repeat from ** 3 more times, sl st to first stitch to join rnd.
Fasten off. Weave in ends.

If you want your little darling to have the cutest shoes, then look no further! These are super sweet and a blast to crochet!

Finished Measurements
Children's Small: 5.5"/14 cm long, 2"/5 cm wide
Children's Medium: 6.5"/16.5 cm long, 2"/5 cm wide
Children's Large: 7.5"/19 cm long, 2.5"/6 cm wide

Yarn
- Red Heart Soft, medium worsted weight #4 yarn, 100% acrylic (256 yd/234 m, 5 oz/142 g per skein)
  1 skein #9779 Berry (Color A)
  1 skein #4601 Off White (Color B)

Hook and Other Materials
- US G-6/4.25 mm crochet hook or size to obtain gauge
- 4 stitch markers
- Yarn needle

Gauge
16 sts and 20 rows in sc = 4"/10 cm square

Notes
- You will crochet two soles for each slipper, then sew them together. The heel and toe are then crocheted onto the sole.
- For a tutorial on Single Crochet Decrease (sc dec) and Half Double Crochet Decrease (hdc dec), see pages 87 and 88.

Attach the tie to the center stitch of the toe.

Sole (make 4)
Small
Using Color A, ch5.
Row 1: Turn, sc in second chain from hook and in each across (4 sts).
Row 2: Turn, ch1, 2sc in first stitch, sc2, 2sc in next stitch (6 sts).
Rows 3–7: Turn, ch1, sc in each stitch.
NOTE: Mark Row 7 with stitch marker on each side.
Row 8: Turn, sc dec, sc2, sc dec (4 sts).
Row 9: Turn, ch1, 2sc in first stitch, sc2, 2sc in next stitch (6 sts).
Row 10: Turn, ch1, 2sc in first stitch, sc4, 2sc in next stitch (8 sts).
Rows 11–13: Turn, ch1, sc in each stitch.
Row 14: Turn, 2sc in first stitch, sc6, 2sc in next stitch (10 sts).
NOTE: Mark Row 14 with stitch marker on each side.
Rows 15–17: Turn, ch1, sc in each stitch.
Row 18: Turn, sc dec, sc6, sc dec (8 sts).
Row 19: Turn, ch1, sc in each stitch.
Row 20: Turn, sc dec, sc4, sc dec (6 sts).
Row 21: Turn, ch1, sc in each stitch.
Row 22: Turn, sc dec, sc2, sc dec (4 sts).
Fasten off. Weave in ends.
Using yarn needle, sew 2 soles together around the edge to create one sole for each sandal.

Medium
Using Color A, ch5.
Row 1: Turn, sc in second chain from hook and in each across (4 sts).
Row 2: Turn, ch1, 2sc in first stitch, sc4, 2sc in next stitch (6 sts).
Rows 3–9: Turn, ch1, sc in each stitch.
NOTE: Mark Row 9 with stitch marker on each side.
Row 10: Turn, sc dec, sc2, sc dec (4 sts).
Row 11: Turn, ch1, 2sc in first stitch, sc2, 2sc in next stitch (6 sts).
Row 12: Turn, ch1, 2sc in first stitch, sc4, 2sc in next stitch (8 sts).
Rows 13–15: Turn, ch1, sc in each stitch.
NOTE: Mark Row 14 with stitch marker on each side.
Row 16: Turn, 2sc in first stitch, sc6, 2sc in next stitch (10 sts).
Rows 17–21: Turn, ch1, sc in each stitch.
Row 22: Turn, sc dec, sc6, sc dec (8 sts).
Row 23: Turn, ch1, sc in each stitch.
Row 24: Turn, sc dec, sc4, sc dec (6 sts).

Row 25: Turn, ch1, sc in each stitch.
Row 26: Turn, sc dec, sc2, sc dec (4 sts).
Row 27: Turn, ch1, sc in each stitch.
Fasten off. Weave in ends.
Using yarn needle, sew 2 soles together around the edge to create one sole for each sandal.

Large
Using Color A, ch6.
Row 1: Turn, sc in second chain from hook and in each across (5 sts).
Row 2: Turn, ch1, 2sc in first stitch, sc3, 2sc in next stitch (7 sts).
Rows 3–10: Turn, ch1, sc in each stitch.
NOTE: Mark Row 10 with stitch marker on each side.
Row 11: Turn, sc dec, sc2, sc dec (5 sts).
Row 12: Turn, ch1, 2sc in first stitch, sc3, 2sc in next stitch (7 sts).
Row 13: Turn, ch1, 2sc in first stitch, sc5, 2sc in next stitch (9 sts).
Rows 14–17: Turn, ch1, sc in each stitch.
NOTE: Mark Row 16 with stitch marker on each side.
Row 18: Turn, 2sc in first stitch, sc7, 2sc in next stitch (11 sts).
Rows 19–23: Turn, ch1, sc in each stitch.
Row 24: Turn, sc dec, sc7, sc dec (9 sts).
Row 25: Turn, ch1, sc in each stitch.
Row 26: Turn, sc dec, sc5, sc dec (7 sts).
Row 27: Turn, ch1, sc in each stitch.
Row 28: Turn, sc dec, sc3, sc dec (5 sts).
Row 29: Turn, ch1, sc in each stitch.
Fasten off. Weave in ends.
Using yarn needle, sew 2 soles together around the edge to create one sole for each sandal.

Heel for All Sizes
Row 1: With the heel of the sole closest to you, join yarn at closest stitch marker on right, ch1, using ends of rows as stitches, sl st to opposite stitch marker.
Rows 2–5: Turn, sc in each stitch.
Row 6: Turn, ch2, dc in each stitch.
Row 7: Turn, sc in each stitch.
Fasten off. Weave in ends.

Toe
Small
Row 1: With the heel closest to you, join yarn in stitch marker at top left, ch2 (does not count as a stitch), using ends of rows as stitches, hdc24 to the next stitch marker (24 sts).
Row 2: Ch2, *hdc, hdc dec, repeat from * 7 more times (16 sts).
Row 3: Ch2, hdc dec 8 times (8 sts).
Row 4: Ch2, *skip 1 stitch, yarn over, insert in next stitch, yarn over and pull through, yarn over and pull through first 2 loops on hook. Keep last loop on hook. Repeat from * 2 more times, yarn over, pull through all loops on hook, dc in last stitch.
Fasten off. Weave in ends.

Medium and Large
Row 1: With heel closest to you, join yarn in stitch marker at top left, ch2 (does not count as a stitch), using ends of rows as stitches, hdc32 to the next stitch marker (32 sts).
Row 2: Ch2, *hdc, hdc dec, repeat from * 10 more times (22 sts).
Row 3: Ch2, hdc dec 11 times (11 sts).
Row 4: Ch2, *skip 1 stitch, yarn over, insert in next stitch, yarn over and pull through, yarn over and pull through first 2 loops on hook. Keep last loop on hook. Repeat from * 3 more times, yarn over, pull through all loops on hook, dc in last stitch.
Fasten off. Weave in ends.

Tie for All Sizes (make 2)
Using Color B, ch110–120 (depends on your preference for bow length).
Fasten off. Weave in ends.
Starting in the center stitch of the toe, pull center of tie through, pull ends through loop, and tighten. Weave in and out of dc row back to the center of the heel on each side. Tie in back.

After weaving the ends of the tie through the double crochet row of the heel on either side, make a bow at the back.

Show off your pedicure or enjoy a walk on the beach in these stylish barefoot sandals. They work up quickly and make a great gift!

Finished Measurements
6"/15.25 cm long, 3.5"/9 cm wide

Yarn
- Aunt Lydia's Crochet Thread Classic 10, 100% mercerized cotton (300 yd/275 m per skein)
  1 skein #495 Wood Violet

Hook and Other Materials
- US C-2/2.75 mm crochet hook or size to obtain gauge
- Yarn needle

Gauge
20 sts and 20 rows in sc = 4"/10 cm square

Notes
- Each sandal is worked from the toe ring up.
- The ch3 at the beginning of the row is counted as the first stitch. The ch1 is not counted as a stitch.

Sandal (make 2)
Ch20, sl st to first chain to join into ring.
Row 1: Ch1, 2sc in ring (2 sts).
Row 2: Turn, ch1, 2sc in each stitch (4 sts).
Row 3: Turn, ch1, 2sc, ch2, skip 2 stitches, 2sc in last stitch (6 sts).
Row 4: Turn, ch3 (counts as first dc stitch), dc in same stitch, ch4, skip 4 stitches, 2dc in last stitch (8 sts).
Row 5: Turn, ch1, 2sc, ch6, skip 6 stitches, 2sc in last stitch (10 sts).
Row 6: Turn, ch3, dc in same stitch, ch8, skip 8 stitches, 2dc in last stitch (12 sts).
Row 7: Turn, ch1, 2sc, ch10, skip 10 stitches, 2sc in last stitch (14 sts).
Row 8: Turn, ch3, dc in same stitch, ch12, skip 12 stitches, 2dc in last stitch (16 sts).
Row 9: Turn, ch1, 2sc, ch14, skip 14 stitches, 2sc in last stitch (18 sts).
Row 10: Turn, ch3, dc in same stitch, ch16, skip 16 stitches, 2dc in last stitch (20 sts).
Row 11: Turn, ch1, 2sc, ch18, skip 18 stitches, 2sc in last stitch (22 sts).
Row 12: Turn, ch3, dc in same stitch, ch20, skip 20 stitches, 2dc in last stitch (24 sts).
Row 13: Turn, ch1, 2sc, ch22, skip 22 stitches, 2sc in last stitch (26 sts).
Row 14: Turn, ch3, dc in same stitch, ch24, skip 24 stitches, 2dc in last stitch (28 sts).
Row 15: Turn, ch1, 2sc, ch24, skip 24 stitches, 2sc in last stitch.
Fasten off. Weave in ends.

Finishing and Straps
Ch75 for the first strap, 2sc in first stitch in the top corner of the last row of sandal to join, ch26, skip 26 stitches, 2sc in last stitch of the top row, ch76 for the second strap.
Repeat for second sandal.
Fasten off. Weave in ends.

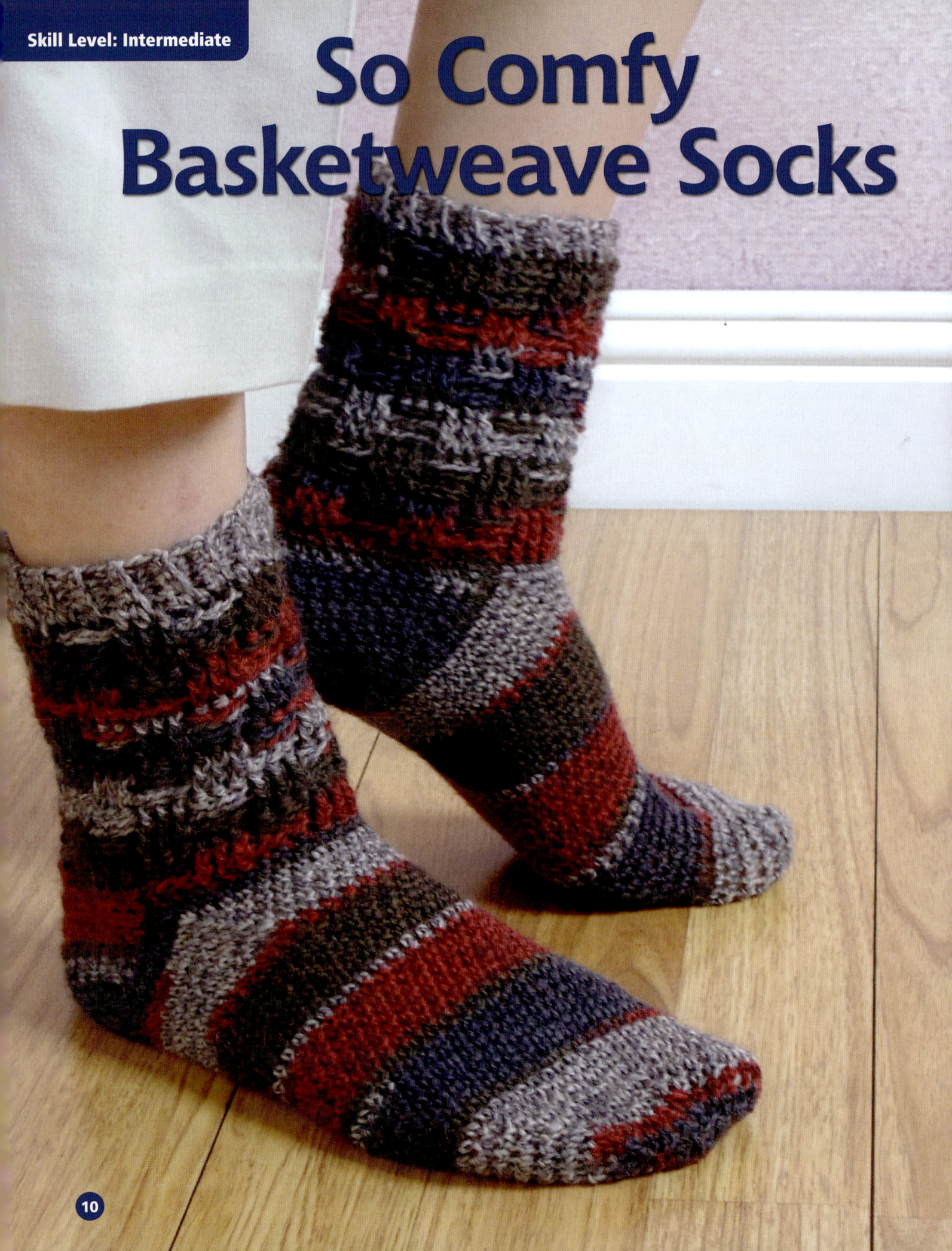

Skill Level: Intermediate

So Comfy Basketweave Socks

Snuggle up in a pair of the softest socks and know that you made them! Crocheted using a self-striping yarn, you'll have a fashionable pair of socks in no time!

Finished Measurements
Women's Small: 8"/20.5 cm long, 3.5"/8.9 cm wide
Women's Medium: 9"/23 cm long, 4"/10 cm wide
Women's Large: 10"/25.5 cm long, 4"/10 cm wide

Yarn
- Patons Kroy Socks, super fine weight #1 yarn, 75% wool/25% nylon (166 yd/152 m, 1.75 oz/50 g per skein) 2 skeins #55048 Grey Brown Marl

Hook and Other Materials
- US E-4/3.5 mm crochet hook or size to obtain gauge
- Yarn needle
- Stitch marker (optional)

Gauge
20 sts and 24 rows in sc = 4"/10 cm square

Notes
- The sock is worked in five sections from the cuff down.
- The leg, gusset, and foot sections are worked continuously in the round. If you like, locate the beginning of the round with a stitch marker.
- The heel is worked seamlessly into the sock. After creating the heel, you will move directly into the gusset, using the ends of the rows as stitches.
- For tutorials on Single Crochet Decrease (sc dec), Front Post Double Crochet (fpdc), and Back Post Double Crochet (bpdc), see pages 87, 94, and 96.

Small (make 2)
Cuff
Ch4.
Row 1: Turn, sc3 (3 sts).
Rows 2–36: Turn, ch1, working in back loop only, sc across.
Fasten off, leaving a long tail.
Using yarn needle, sew ends together.

Leg
Rnd 1: Join yarn at seam of Cuff. Using ends of rows as stitches, ch2, dc in each stitch (36 sts).
Rnds 2–4: Working continuously in the round, *fpdc3, bpdc3, repeat from * to complete rnd.
Rnds 5–7: *Bpdc3, fpdc3, repeat from * to complete rnd (36 sts).
Rnds 8–19: (Repeat Rnds 2–7) 2 times.

Heel
Row 1: Sc18 (18 sts).
Rows 2–9: Ch1, turn, sc18.
Row 10: Turn, ch1, sc, sc dec, sc12, sc dec, sc (16 sts).
Row 11: Turn, ch1, sc, sc dec, sc10, sc dec, sc (14 sts).
Row 12: Turn, ch1, sc, sc dec, sc8, sc dec, sc (12 sts).
Row 13: Turn, ch1, sc, sc dec, sc6, sc dec, sc (10 sts).
Row 14: Turn, ch1, sc, sc dec, sc4, sc dec, sc (8 sts).
Row 15: Turn, ch1, sc, sc dec, sc2, sc dec, sc (6 sts).
Row 16: Turn, ch1, sc, sc dec, sc dec, sc (4 sts).

Gusset
Rnd 1: Working continuously in the round and using the ends of rows as stitches, sc14, sc dec, sc18, sc dec, sc18 (52 sts).
Rnd 2: Sc13, sc dec, sc21, sc dec, sc17 (50 sts).
Rnd 3: Sc12, sc dec, sc21, sc dec, sc16 (48 sts).
Rnd 4: Sc11, sc dec, sc21, sc dec, sc15 (46 sts).
Rnd 5: Sc10, sc dec, sc21, sc dec, sc14 (44 sts).
Rnd 6: Sc9, sc dec, sc21, sc dec, sc13 (42 sts).
Rnd 7: Sc8, sc dec, sc21, sc dec, sc12 (40 sts).
Rnd 8: Sc7, sc dec, sc21, sc dec, sc11 (38 sts).
Rnd 9: Sc6, sc dec, sc21, sc dec, sc10 (36 sts).

Foot
Rnds 1–27: Sc in each stitch around.
Rnd 28: *Sc4, sc dec, repeat from * to complete rnd (30 sts).
Rnd 29: *Sc3, sc dec, repeat from * to complete rnd (24 sts).
Rnd 30: *Sc2, sc dec, repeat from * to complete rnd (18 sts).
Fasten off, leaving a long tail.
Using yarn needle, sew toe closed in line with heel. Weave in all ends.

Medium (make 2)
Cuff
Ch4.
Row 1: Turn, sc3 (3 sts).
Rows 2–42: Turn, ch1, working in back loop only, sc across.
Fasten off, leaving a long tail.
Using yarn needle, sew ends together.

Leg
Rnd 1: Join yarn at seam of Cuff. Using ends of rows as stitches, ch2, dc in each stitch (42 sts).
Rnds 2–4: Working continuously in the round, *fpdc3, bpdc3, repeat from * to complete rnd (42 sts).
Rnds 5–7: *Bpdc3, fpdc3, repeat from * to complete rnd (42 sts).
Rnds 8–19: (Repeat Rnds 2–7) 2 times.

Heel
Row 1: Sc21 (21 sts).
Rows 2–9: Ch1, turn, sc21.
Row 10: Turn, ch1, sc, sc dec, sc15, sc dec, sc (19 sts).
Row 11: Turn, ch1, sc, sc dec, sc13, sc dec, sc (17 sts).
Row 12: Turn, ch1, sc, sc dec, sc11, sc dec, sc (15 sts).
Row 13: Turn, ch1, sc, sc dec, sc 9, sc dec, sc (13 sts).
Row 14: Turn, ch1, sc, sc dec, sc7, sc dec, sc (11 sts).
Row 15: Turn, ch1, sc, sc dec, sc5, sc dec, sc (9 sts).
Row 16: Turn, ch1, sc, sc dec, sc3, sc dec, sc (7 sts).
Row 17: Turn, ch1, sc, sc dec, sc, sc dec, sc (5 sts).

Gusset
Rnd 1: Working continuously in the round, sc15, sc dec, sc21, sc dec, sc20 (58 sts).
Rnd 2: Sc14, sc dec, sc21, sc dec, sc19 (56 sts).
Rnd 3: Sc13, sc dec, sc21, sc dec, sc18 (54 sts).
Rnd 4: Sc12, sc dec, sc21, sc dec, sc17 (52 sts).
Rnd 5: Sc11, sc dec, sc21, sc dec, sc16 (50 sts).
Rnd 6: Sc10, sc dec, sc21, sc dec, sc15 (48 sts).
Rnd 7: Sc9, sc dec, sc21, sc dec, sc14 (46 sts).
Rnd 8: Sc8, sc dec, sc21, sc dec, sc13 (44 sts).
Rnd 9: Sc7, sc dec, sc21, sc dec, sc12 (42 sts).

Foot
Rnds 1–27: Sc in each stitch around.
Rnd 28: *Sc5, sc dec, repeat from * to complete rnd (35 sts).
Rnd 29: *Sc4, sc dec, repeat from * to complete rnd (28 sts).
Rnd 30: *Sc3, sc dec, repeat from * to complete rnd (21 sts).
Fasten off, leaving a long tail.
Using yarn needle, sew toe closed in line with heel. Weave in all ends.

Large (make 2)
Cuff
Ch4.
Row 1: Turn, sc3 (3 sts).
Rows 2–48: Turn, ch1, working in back loop only, sc3.
Fasten off, leaving a long tail.
Using yarn needle, sew ends together.

Leg
Rnd 1: Join yarn at seam of Cuff. Using ends of rows as stitches, ch2, dc in each stitch (48 sts).
Rnds 2–4: Working continuously in the round, *fpdc3, bpdc3, repeat from * to complete rnd.
Rnds 5–7: *Bpdc3, fpdc3, repeat from * to complete rnd.
Rnds 8–19: (Repeat Rnds 2–7) 2 times.

Heel
Row 1: Sc24 (24 sts).
Rows 2–11: Ch1, turn, sc24.
Row 12: Turn, ch1, sc, sc dec, sc16, sc dec, sc (22 sts).
Row 13: Turn, ch1, sc, sc dec, sc14, sc dec, sc (20 sts).
Row 14: Turn, ch1, sc, sc dec, sc12, sc dec, sc (18 sts).
Row 15: Turn, ch1, sc, sc dec, sc10, sc dec, sc (16 sts).
Row 16: Turn, ch1, sc, sc dec, sc8, sc dec, sc (14 sts).
Row 17: Turn, ch1, sc, sc dec, sc6, sc dec, sc (12 sts).
Row 18: Turn, ch1, sc, sc dec, sc4, sc dec, sc (10 sts).
Row 19: Turn, ch1, sc, sc dec, sc2, sc dec, sc (8 sts).
Row 20: Turn, ch1, sc, sc dec, sc, sc dec, sc (6 sts).

Gusset
Rnd 1: Working continuously in the round, sc17, sc dec, sc24, sc dec, sc23 (66 sts).
Rnd 2: Sc16, sc dec, sc24, sc dec, sc22 (64 sts).
Rnd 3: Sc15, sc dec, sc24, sc dec, sc21 (62 sts).
Rnd 4: Sc14, sc dec, sc24, sc dec, sc20 (60 sts).
Rnd 5: Sc13, sc dec, sc24, sc dec, sc19 (58 sts).
Rnd 6: Sc12, sc dec, sc24, sc dec, sc18 (56 sts).
Rnd 7: Sc11, sc dec, sc24, sc dec, sc17 (54 sts).
Rnd 8: Sc10, sc dec, sc24, sc dec, sc16 (52 sts).
Rnd 9: Sc9, sc dec, sc24, sc dec, sc15 (50 sts).
Rnd 10: Sc8, sc dec, sc24, sc dec, sc14 (48 sts).

Foot
Rnds 1–31: Sc in each stitch around.
Rnd 32: *Sc6, sc dec, repeat from * to complete rnd (42 sts).
Rnd 33: *Sc5, sc dec, repeat from * to complete rnd (32 sts).
Rnd 34: *Sc4, sc dec, repeat from * to complete rnd (24 sts).
Rnd 35: *Sc3, sc dec, repeat from * to complete rnd (18 sts).
Fasten off, leaving a long tail.
Using yarn needle, sew toe closed flat in line with heel. Weave in all ends.

This fun twist on the house scuff will be a huge hit with all your girly girl friends and family!

Slip stitching the two soles together with Color A creates a decorative border all around the sole.

Finished Measurements

Women's Small: 8"/20.5 cm long, 3.5"/8.9 cm wide
Women's Medium: 9"/23 cm long, 4"/10 cm wide
Women's Large: 10"/25.5 cm long, 4"/10 cm wide

Yarn

- Bernat Softee Chunky, super bulky #6 yarn, 100% acrylic (108 yd/99 m, 3.5 oz/100 g per skein)
  1 skein #16112828005 White (Color A)
- Yarn Bee Soft Illusion, super bulky #6 yarn, 65% acrylic/35% polyamide (87 yd/80 m, 4 oz/115 g per skein)
  1 skein #100 Islander (Color B)
- Bernat Vickie Howell Sheep(ish), 70% acrylic/30% wool (167 yd/ 153 m, 3 oz/85 g per skein)
  1 skein #16416900014 Turquoise(ish) (Color C)
  1 skein #16416900007 Hot Pink(ish) (Color D)

Hook and Other Materials

- US H-8/5.0 mm crochet hook or size to obtain gauge
- Yarn needle

Gauge

Using Color A, 12 sts and 14 rows in sc = 4"/10 cm square

Notes

- The slipper is worked in three separate sections: sole, top, and flowers.
- The soles are crocheted in joined rounds from the center out. You will crochet two soles per slipper and sew them together, then add the top of the scuff and the flowers.
- For a tutorial on Single Crochet Decrease (sc dec), see page 87.

Small

Sole (make 4)

Using Color A, ch15.

Rnd 1: Turn, sc in second chain from hook, sc4, sl st 2, sc2, hdc2, dc2, 6dc in last chain, working continuously onto opposite side of chain, dc2, hdc2, sc2, sl st 2, sc5, sl st to first stitch to join rnd (32 sts).

Rnd 2: Ch1, 2sc in same stitch, sc4, sl st 2, sc2, hdc4, 2hdc in next 6 stitches, hdc4, sc2, sl st 2, sc4, 2sc in last stitch, sl st to first stitch to join rnd (40 sts).

Rnd 3: Ch1, 2sc in same stitch, 2sc in next stitch, sc8, hdc4, (hdc, 2hdc in next stitch) 6 times, hdc4, sc8, 2sc in last 2 stitches, sl st to first stitch to join rnd (50 sts).

Rnd 4: Ch1, sc in same stitch, 2sc in next 2 stitches, sc7, hdc6, (hdc2, 2hdc in next stitch) 6 times, hdc6, sc7, 2sc in next 2 stitches, sc in last stitch, sl st to first stitch to join rnd (60 sts).

Fasten off. Weave in ends.

Top (make 2)

Using Color B, ch14.

Row 1: Turn, sc in second chain from hook and in each chain across (13 sts).
Row 2: Turn, ch1, sc13.
Row 3: Turn, ch1, sc12, 2sc in last stitch (14 sts).
Row 4: Turn, ch1, 2sc in next stitch, sc13 (15 sts).
Row 5: Turn, ch1, sc14, 2sc in last stitch (16 sts).
Rows 6–10: Ch1, sc16.
Row 11: Turn, ch1, sc14, sc dec (15 sts).
Row 12: Turn, sc dec, sc13 (14 sts).
Row 13: Turn, sc12, sc dec (13 sts).
Row 14: Turn, ch1, sc13.
Fasten off. Weave in ends.

Medium
Sole (make 4)

Using Color A, ch18.

Rnd 1: Turn, sc in second chain from hook, sc5, sl st 2, sc2, hdc3, dc3, 6dc in last chain, working continuously onto opposite side of chain, dc3, hdc3, sc2, sl st 2, sc6, sl st to first stitch to join rnd (36 sts).

Rnd 2: Ch1, 2sc in same stitch, sc5, sl st 2, sc2, hdc6, 2hdc in next 6 stitches, hdc6, sc2, sl st 2, sc5, 2sc in last stitch, sl st to first stitch to join rnd (44 sts).

Rnd 3: Ch1, 2sc in same stitch, 2sc in next stitch, sc10, hdc5, (hdc, 2hdc in next stitch) 6 times, hdc5, sc10, 2sc in last 2 stitches, sl st to first stitch to join rnd (54 sts).

Rnd 4: Ch1, sc in same stitch, 2sc in next 2 stitches, sc9, hdc7, (hdc2, 2hdc in next stitch) 6 times, hdc7, sc9, 2sc in next 2 stitches, sc in last stitch, sl st to first stitch to join rnd (64 sts).

Fasten off. Weave in ends.

Top (make 2)

Using Color B, ch14.

Row 1: Turn, sc in second chain from hook and in each chain across (13 sts).
Row 2: Turn, ch1, sc13.
Row 3: Turn, ch1, sc12, 2sc in last stitch (14 sts).
Row 4: Turn, ch1, 2sc, sc13 (15 sts).
Row 5: Turn, ch1, sc14, 2sc in last stitch (16 sts).
Rows 6–10: Ch1, sc16.
Row 11: Turn, ch1, sc14, sc dec (15 sts).
Row 12: Turn, sc dec, sc13 (14 sts).
Row 13: Turn, sc12, sc dec (13 sts).
Row 14: Turn, ch1, sc13.
Fasten off. Weave in ends.

Large
Sole (make 4)

Using Color A, ch20.

Rnd 1: Turn, sc in second chain from hook, sc6, sl st 2, sc2, hdc3, dc4, 6dc in last chain, working continuously onto opposite side of chain, dc4, hdc3, sc2, sl st 2, sc7, sl st to first stitch to join rnd (42 sts).

Rnd 2: Ch1, 2sc in same stitch, sc6, sl st 2, sc2, hdc7, 2hdc in next 6 stitches, hdc7, sc2, sl st 2, sc6, 2sc in last stitch, sl st to first stitch to join rnd (50 sts).

Rnd 3: Ch1, 2sc in same stitch, 2sc in next stitch, sc11, hdc6, (hdc, 2hdc in next stitch) 6 times, hdc6, sc11, 2sc in last 2 stitches, sl st to first stitch to join rnd (60 sts).

Rnd 4: Ch1, sc in same stitch, 2sc in next 2 stitches, sc8, hdc10, (hdc2, 2hdc in next stitch) 6 times, hdc10, sc8, 2sc in next 2 stitches, sc in last stitch, sl st to first stitch to join rnd (70 sts).

Fasten off. Weave in ends.

Top (make 2)

Using Color B, ch16.

Row 1: Turn, sc in second chain from hook and in each chain across (15 sts).
Row 2: Turn, ch1, sc15.
Row 3: Turn, ch1, sc14, 2sc in last stitch (16 sts).
Row 4: Turn, ch1, 2sc, sc15 (17 sts).
Row 5: Turn, ch1, sc16, 2sc in last stitch (18 sts).
Rows 6–10: Ch1, sc18 (18 sts).
Row 11: Turn, ch1, sc16, sc dec (17 sts).
Row 12: Turn, sc dec, sc15 (16 sts).
Row 13: Turn, sc13, sc dec (15 sts).
Row 14: Turn, ch1, sc15.
Fasten off. Weave in ends.

Flowers for All Sizes

Back (make 2)
Using Color C, ch4, sl st to first chain to create a ring.

Rnd 1: Ch1, 10sc in ring (10 sts).

Rnd 2: Ch1, sc, *ch4, skip 1 stitch, sc in next stitch, repeat from * to complete rnd.

Rnd 3: Ch1, sc in first ch4 space, dc in main center ring, 8dc in ch4 space from Rnd 2, *sc in next ch4 space, dc in main center ring, 8dc in ch4 space from Rnd 2, repeat from * to complete rnd, sl st to first stitch to join.

Fasten off. Weave in ends.

Top (make 2)
Using Color D, ch20.

Row 1: Turn, sc in second chain from hook and in each across (19 sts).

Fasten off, leaving a long tail.

Roll strip into a small rosette and, using yarn needle, sew and secure.

To finish, using yarn needle, sew the top and back together in the center.

Back of the sole

Finishing

Hold 2 soles wrong sides together and, using yarn needle and Color A, slip stitch them together using the last row.

Fasten off. Weave in ends.

Using Color B, whip stitch the top into place on the sole.

Fasten off. Weave in ends.

Decide which scuff will be the right and which the left. Position a flower on each scuff so that it is to the outside of the slipper, then, using Color D, sew it in place. Weave in the end.

Repeat for the other scuff.

What more could you ask for than rainbows and ruffles? Get your color and cuteness fix with this fun crochet pattern. By using the basic chain stitch, you can create a ruffle rainbow! This is a great way to make use of yarn left over from other projects.

Finished Measurements
Children's Small: 6"/15.25 cm long, 2"/5 cm wide
Children's Medium: 7"/17.75 cm long, 2.5"/6 cm wide
Children's Large: 8"/20.25 cm long, 2.5"/6 cm wide

Yarn
- Red Heart Soft, medium worsted weight #4 yarn, 100% acrylic (256 yd/234 m, 5 oz/141 g per skein)
    1 skein #4600 White (Color A)
    1 skein #4608 Wine (Color B)
    1 skein #4422 Tangerine (Color C)
    1 skein #9114 Honey (Color D)
    1 skein #4420 Guacamole (Color E)
    1 skein #2515 Turquoise (Color F)
    1 skein #9518 Teal (Color G)
    1 skein #3729 Grape (Color H)

Hook and Other Materials
- US F-5/3.75 mm crochet hook or size to obtain gauge
- Yarn needle

Gauge
16 sts and 12 rows in sc = 4"/10 cm square

Notes
- The slipper is worked in joined rounds from the center of the sole out.
- You will not count the first ch1 or the last sl st as a stitch.
- For tutorials on Single Crochet Decrease (sc dec) and Front Post Double Crochet Decrease (fpdc dec), see pages 87 and 94.

Small (make 2)

Using Color A, ch14.
Rnd 1: Turn, sc in second chain from hook, sc3, hdc3, dc5, 6dc in last chain, working continuously onto opposite side of chain, dc5, hdc3, sc4, sl st to first stitch to join rnd (30 sts).
Rnd 2: Ch1, 2sc in same stitch, sc3, hdc4, dc4, 2dc in next 6 stitches, dc4, hdc4, sc3, 2sc in last stitch, sl st to first stitch to join rnd (38 sts).
Rnd 3: Ch1, sc in same stitch, 2sc in next stitch, sc3, hdc8, (hdc, 2hdc in next stitch) 6 times, hdc8, sc3, 2sc next stitch, sc in last stitch, sl st to first stitch to join rnd (46 sts).
Rnd 4: Ch1, sc in same stitch, sc in next stitch, 2sc in next stitch, sc3, hdc8, (hdc2, 2hdc in next stitch) 6 times, hdc8, sc3, sc2, sl st to first stitch to join rnd (54 sts).
Rnd 5: Ch2, working in back loop only, dc in each stitch, sl st to first stitch to join rnd.
Rnd 6: Ch2, fpdc15, (fpdc2, fpdc dec) 6 times, fpdc19, sl st to first stitch to join rnd (48 sts).
Rnd 7: Ch2, fpdc15, (fpdc, fpdc dec) 6 times, fpdc19, sl st to first stitch to join rnd (42 sts).
Rnd 8: Ch2, fpdc15, fpdc dec 6 times, fpdc15, sl st to first stitch to join (36 sts).
Rnd 9: Ch2, fpdc11, fpdc dec 3 times, dc, fpdc dec 3 times, fpdc11, sl st to first stitch to join rnd (30 sts).

Rnd 10: Ch2, fpdc11, fpdc dec 2 times, fpdc11, sl st to first stitch to join rnd (28 sts).

Rnds 11–17: Ch2, working in back loop only, dc in each stitch, sl st to first stitch to join rnd.

Fasten off. Weave in ends.

Medium (make 2)

Using Color A, ch18.

Rnd 1: Turn, sc in second chain from hook, sc5, hdc4, dc6, 6dc in last chain, working continuously onto opposite side of chain, dc6, hdc4, sc6, sl st to first stitch to join rnd (38 sts).

Rnd 2: Ch1, 2sc in same stitch, sc5, hdc6, dc4, 2dc in next 6 stitches, dc4, hdc6, sc5, 2sc in last stitch, sl st to first stitch to join rnd (46 sts).

Rnd 3: Ch1, sc in same stitch, 2sc in next stitch, sc4, hdc11, (hdc, 2hdc in next stitch) 6 times, hdc11, sc4, 2sc next stitch, sc in last stitch, sl st to first stitch to join rnd (54 sts).

Rnd 4: Ch1, sc in same stitch, sc in next stitch, 2sc in next stitch, sc4, hdc11, (hdc2, 2hdc in next stitch) 6 times, hdc11, sc4, 2sc in next stitch, sc2, sl st to first stitch to join rnd (62 sts).

Rnd 5: Ch2, working in back loop only, dc in each stitch, sl st to first stitch to join rnd.

Rnd 6: Ch2, fpdc19, (fpdc2, fpdc dec) 6 times, fpdc19, sl st to first stitch to join rnd (56 sts).

Rnd 7: Ch2, fpdc19, (fpdc, fpdc dec) 6 times, fpdc19, sl st to first stitch to join rnd (50 sts).

Rnd 8: Ch2, fpdc19, fpdc dec 6 times, fpdc19, sl st to first stitch to join rnd (44 sts).

Rnd 9: Ch2, fpdc15, fpdc dec 3 times, dc, fpdc dec 3 times, fpdc15, sl st to first stitch to join rnd (40 sts).

Rnd 10: Ch2, fpdc15, fpdc dec 2 times, fpdc15, sl st to first stitch to join rnd (38 sts).

Rnds 11–17: Ch2, working in back loop only, dc in each stitch, sl st to first stitch to join rnd.

Fasten off. Weave in ends.

Large (make 2)

Using Color A, ch22.

Rnd 1: Turn, sc in second chain from hook, sc7, hdc4, dc8, 6dc in last chain, working continuously onto opposite side of chain, dc8, hdc4, sc8, sl st to first stitch to join rnd (46 sts).

Rnd 2: Ch1, 2sc in same stitch, sc6, hdc6, dc7, 2dc in next 6 stitches, dc7, hdc6, sc6, 2sc in last stitch, sl st to first stitch to join rnd (54 sts).

Rnd 3: Ch1, sc in same stitch, 2sc in next stitch, sc4, hdc15, (hdc, 2hdc in next stitch) 6 times, hdc15, sc4, 2sc next stitch, sc in last stitch, sl st to first stitch to join rnd (62 sts).

Rnd 4: Ch1, sc in same stitch, sc in next stitch, 2sc in next stitch, sc4, hdc15, (hdc2, 2hdc in next stitch) 6 times, hdc15, sc4, 2sc in next stitch, sc2, sl st to first stitch to join rnd (70 sts).

Rnd 5: Ch2, working in back loop only, dc in each stitch, sl st to first stitch to join rnd.

Rnd 6: Ch2, fpdc23, (fpdc2, fpdc dec) 6 times, fpdc23, sl st to first stitch to join rnd (64 sts).

Rnd 7: Ch2, fpdc23, (fpdc, fpdc dec) 6 times, fpdc23, sl st to first stitch to join rnd (58 sts).

Rnd 8: Ch2, fpdc23, fpdc dec 6 times, fpdc23, sl st to first stitch to join rnd (52 sts).

Rnd 9: Ch2, fpdc19, fpdc dec 3 times, dc, fpdc dec 3 times, fpdc19, sl st to first stitch to join rnd (46 sts).

Rnd 10: Ch2, fpdc19, fpdc dec 2 times, fpdc19, sl st to first stitch to join rnd (42 sts).

Rnds 11–17: Ch2, working in back loop only, dc in each stitch, sl st to first stitch to join rnd.

Fasten off. Weave in ends.

Ruffles for All Sizes

Join Color B at the sl st of Rnd 11 in the exposed loop created by working in the back loop only, ch3, sl st to same stitch, *ch3, sl st to next stitch, repeat from * to complete rnd. Cut Color B.

Join Color C at the sl st of Rnd 12 in the exposed loop created by working in the back loop only, ch3, sl st to same stitch, *ch3, sl st to next stitch, repeat from * to complete rnd. Cut Color C.

Repeat for Colors D, E, F, G, and H on Rnds 13–17, joining each color at the beginning of the rnd and cutting it at the end of the rnd. Weave in all ends.

These beautiful tailored socks require only basic stitches. Wear them as slippers around the house or outside with clogs or mules for a casual look.

Finished Measurements
Women's Small: 8"/20.5 cm long, 3.5"/8.9 cm wide
Women's Medium: 9"/23 cm long, 4"/10 cm wide
Women's Large: 10"/25.5 cm long, 4"/10 cm wide

Yarn
- Bernat Softee Baby, light worsted weight #3 yarn, 100% acrylic (362 yd/331 m, 5 oz/140 g per skein) 1 skein #30410 Soft Peach

Hook and Other Materials
- C-2/2.75 mm crochet hook or size to obtain gauge
- Stitch marker
- Yarn needle

Gauge
20 sts and 20 rows in sc = 4"/10 cm square

Notes
- Each slipper is worked in sections: The cuff is crocheted in rows, then sewn together. Yarn is joined at the cuff and the leg is worked in joined rounds. The heel is worked, then the gusset and foot are crocheted continuously in the round.
- The toe section of the sock is sewn together at the end.
- For a tutorial on Single Crochet Decrease (sc dec), see page 87.

Small (make 2)
Cuff
Ch8.
Row 1: Sc in second chain from hook and in each across (7 sts).
Rows 2–30: Turn, ch1, working in back loop only, sc in each stitch.
Fasten off, leaving a long tail.
Using yarn needle, sew ends together.

Leg
Rnd 1: Join yarn at seam of Cuff, ch2, using the ends of rows as stitches, skip 2 stitches, *(dc3, ch2, dc) in next stitch, skip 3 stitches, repeat from * to complete rnd, sl st to first ch2 to join (30 sts).
Rnds 2–5: Turn, ch2, (dc3, ch2, dc) in each ch2 space, sl st to first ch2 to join rnd.
Rnd 6: Turn, ch4, *sc in ch2 space, sc in next stitch, ch2, repeat from * to complete rnd, sl st to second chain of ch4 to join rnd.

Heel
Rnd 1: Ch1, sc in each stitch.
Rnds 2–7: Turn, ch1, sc15 (15 sts).
Rnd 8: Turn, ch1, sc, sc dec, sc9, sc dec, sc in last stitch (13 sts).
Rnd 9: Turn, ch1, sc, sc dec, sc7, sc dec, sc in last stitch (11 sts).
Rnd 10: Turn, ch1, sc, sc dec, sc5, sc dec, sc in last stitch (9 sts).
Rnd 11: Turn, ch1, sc, sc dec, sc3, sc dec, sc in last stitch (7 sts).
Rnd 12: Turn, ch1, sc, sc dec, sc, sc dec, sc in last stitch (5 sts).

Gusset
Rnd 1: Turn, ch1, using ends of rows of heel as stitches, sc14, sc15 across leg, sc14 down opposite edge of heel, sc5 along bottom of heel, do not join (48 sts).
Rnd 2: Mark first stitch with marker, sc12, sc dec, sc15, sc dec, sc17 (46 sts).
Rnd 3: Working continuously in the round, sc11, sc dec, sc15, sc dec, sc16 (44 sts).
Rnd 4: Sc10, sc dec, sc15, sc dec, sc15 (42 sts).
Rnd 5: Sc9, sc dec, sc15, sc dec, sc14 (40 sts).
Rnd 6: Sc8, sc dec, sc15, sc dec, sc13 (38 sts).
Rnd 7: Sc7, sc dec, sc15, sc dec, sc12 (36 sts).
Rnd 8: Sc6, sc dec, sc15, sc dec, sc11 (34 sts).

Foot
Rnds 1–12: Sc in each stitch.
Rnd 13: Sc15, sc dec, sc15, sc dec (32 sts).
Rnd 14: *Sc6, sc dec, repeat from * to complete rnd (28 sts).
Rnd 15: *Sc5, sc dec, repeat from * to complete rnd (24 sts).
Rnd 16: *Sc4, sc dec, repeat from * to complete rnd (20 sts).
Rnd 17: *Sc3, sc dec, repeat from * to complete rnd (16 sts).
Rnd 18: *Sc2, sc dec, repeat from * to complete rnd (12 sts).
Fasten off, leaving a long tail.

Medium (make 2)

Cuff
Ch8.

Row 1: Sc in second chain from hook and in each across (7 sts).

Rows 2–34: Turn, ch1, working in back loop only, sc in each stitch.

Fasten off, leaving a long tail.

Using yarn needle, sew ends together.

Leg
Rnd 1: Join yarn at Cuff seam, ch2, using ends of rows as stitches, skip 2 stitches, *(dc3, ch2, dc) in next stitch, skip 3 stitches, repeat from * to complete rnd, sl st to the first ch2 to join (34 sts).

Rnds 2–5: Turn, ch2, *(dc3, ch2, dc) in each ch2 space, sl st to ch2 to join rnd.

Rnd 6: Turn, ch4, *sc in ch2 space, sc in next stitch, ch2, repeat from * to complete rnd, sl st to second chain of ch4 to join.

Heel
Rnd 1: Ch1, sc in each stitch.

Rnds 2–9: Turn, ch1, sc17 (17 sts).

Rnd 10: Turn, ch1, sc, sc dec, sc11, sc dec, sc in last stitch (15 sts).

Rnd 11: Turn, ch1, sc, sc dec, sc9, sc dec, sc in last stitch (13 sts).

Rnd 12: Turn, ch1, sc, sc dec, sc7, sc dec, sc in last stitch (11 sts).

Rnd 13: Turn, ch1, sc, sc dec, sc5, sc dec, sc in last stitch (9 sts).

Rnd 14: Turn, ch1, sc, sc dec, sc3, sc dec, sc in last stitch (7 sts).

Rnd 15: Turn, ch1, sc, sc dec, sc, sc dec, sc in last stitch (5 sts).

Gusset
Rnd 1: Turn, ch1, using ends of rows of heel as stitches, sc15, sc17 across leg, sc15 down opposite edge of heel, sc5 along bottom of heel, do not join (52 sts).

Rnd 2: Mark first stitch with marker, sc13, sc dec, sc17, sc dec, sc18 sts (50 sts).

Rnd 3: Working continuously in the round, sc12, sc dec, sc17, sc dec, sc17 (48 sts).

Rnd 4: Sc11, sc dec, sc17, sc dec, sc16 (46 sts).

Rnd 5: Sc10, sc dec, sc17, sc dec, sc15 (44 sts).

Rnd 6: Sc9, sc dec, sc17, sc dec, sc14 (42 sts).

Rnd 7: Sc8, sc dec, sc17, sc dec, sc13 (40 sts).

Rnd 8: Sc7, sc dec, sc17, sc dec, sc12 (38 sts).

Rnd 9: Sc6, sc dec, sc17, sc dec, sc11 (36 sts).

Foot
Rnds 1–14: Sc in each stitch.

Rnd 15: *Sc4, sc dec, repeat from * to complete rnd (30 sts).

Rnd 16: *Sc3, sc dec, repeat from * to complete rnd (24 sts).

Rnd 17: *Sc2, sc dec, repeat from * to complete rnd (18 sts).

Rnd 18: *Sc, sc dec, repeat from * to complete rnd (12 sts).

Fasten off, leaving a long tail.

Large (make 2)

Cuff
Ch8.

Row 1: Sc in second chain from hook and in each across (7 sts).

Rows 2–38: Turn, ch1, working in back loop only, sc in each stitch.

Fasten off, leaving a long tail.

Using yarn needle, sew ends together.

Leg
Rnd 1: Join yarn at Cuff seam, ch2, using the ends of rows as stitches, skip 2 stitches, *(dc3, ch2, dc) in next stitch, skip 3 stitches, repeat from * to complete rnd, sl st to first ch2 to join.

Rnds 2–5: Turn, ch2, *(dc3, ch2, dc) in each ch2 space, sl st to ch2 to join rnd.

Rnd 6: Turn, ch4, *sc in ch2 space, sc in next stitch, ch2, repeat from * to complete rnd, sl st to second chain of ch4 to join.

Heel
Rnd 1: Ch1, sc in each stitch (38 sts).

Rnds 2–9: Turn, ch1, sc19 (19 sts).

Rnd 10: Turn, ch1, sc, sc dec, sc13, sc dec, sc in last stitch (17 sts).

Rnd 11: Turn, ch1, sc, sc dec, sc11, sc dec, sc in last stitch (15 sts).

Rnd 12: Turn, ch1, sc, sc dec, sc9, sc dec, sc in last stitch (13 sts).

Rnd 13: Turn, ch1, sc, sc dec, sc7, sc dec, sc in last stitch (11 sts).

Rnd 14: Turn, ch1, sc, sc dec, sc5, sc dec, sc in last stitch (9 sts).

Rnd 15: Turn, ch1, sc, sc dec, sc3, sc dec, sc in last stitch (7 sts).

Rnd 16: Turn, ch1, sc, sc dec, sc, sc dec, sc in last stitch (5 sts).

Gusset

Rnd 1: Turn, ch1, using ends of rows of heel as stitches, sc15, sc19 across leg, sc15 down opposite edge of heel, sc5 along bottom of heel, do not join (54 sts).

Rnd 2: Mark first stitch with marker, sc13, sc dec, sc19, sc dec, sc20 sts (52 sts).

Rnd 3: Working continuously in the round, sc12, sc dec, sc19, sc dec, sc17 (50 sts).

Rnd 4: Sc11, sc dec, sc19, sc dec, sc16 (48 sts).

Rnd 5: Sc10, sc dec, sc19, sc dec, sc15 (46 sts).

Rnd 6: Sc9, sc dec, sc19, sc dec, sc14 (44 sts).

Rnd 7: Sc8, sc dec, sc19, sc dec, sc13 (42 sts).

Rnd 8: Sc7, sc dec, sc19, sc dec, sc12 (40 sts).

Rnd 9: Sc6, sc dec, sc19, sc dec, sc11 (38 sts).

Foot

Rnds 1–18: Sc in each stitch.

Rnd 2: Sc dec, sc17, sc dec, sc 17 (36 sts).

Rnd 3: *Sc7, sc dec, repeat from * to complete rnd (32 sts).

Rnd 4: *Sc6, sc dec, repeat from * to complete rnd (28 sts).

Rnd 5: *Sc5, sc dec, repeat from * to complete rnd (24 sts).

Rnd 6: *Sc4, sc dec, repeat from * to complete rnd (20 sts).

Rnd 7: *Sc3, sc dec, repeat from * to complete rnd (16 sts).

Fasten off, leaving a long tail.

Finishing for All Sizes

With the wrong side of the slipper sock facing out, use yarn needle and sew toe opening together in alignment with the heel. Weave in ends.

Some classics never go out of style. Crochet a pair of these up for your favorite dad and watch him smile as he slips them on.

Finished Measurements
Men's Small: 9.5"/24.25 cm long, 4"/10 cm wide
Men's Medium: 10.5"/26.75 cm long, 4"/10 cm wide
Men's Large: 11.5"/29.25 cm long, 4"/10 cm wide

Yarn
- Red Heart Super Saver, medium worsted weight #4 yarn, 100% acrylic (364 yd/333 m, 7 oz/189 g per skein) 1 skein #3950 Charcoal

Hook and Other Materials
- US F-5/3.75 mm crochet hook or size to obtain gauge
- Stitch markers
- Yarn needle

Gauge
10 sts x 12 rows in sc = 3"/7.75 cm square

Notes
- The loafer is worked in three sections and then assembled. Two soles are made for each loafer and sewn together. The two side panels are then sewn on and finally the top of the loafer.
- Use stitch markers to line up the side panels to the sole when sewing together.
- For a tutorial on Single Crochet Decrease (sc dec), see page 87.

Small
Sole (make 4)
Ch6.
Row 1: Sc in second chain from hook and in each chain across (5 sts).
Row 2: Turn, ch1, 2sc in next stitch, sc3, 2sc in last stitch (7 sts).
Row 3: Turn, ch1, 2sc in next stitch, sc5, 2sc in last stitch (9 sts).
Rows 4–10: Turn, ch1, sc in each stitch.
Row 11: Turn, sc dec, sc5, sc dec (7 sts).
Row 12: Turn, ch1, sc in each stitch.
Row 13: Turn, ch1, 2sc in next stitch, sc5, 2sc in last stitch (9 sts).
Rows 14–17: Turn, ch1, sc in each stitch.
Row 18: Turn, ch1, 2sc in next stitch , sc7, 2sc in last stitch (11 sts).
Rows 19–22: Turn, ch1, sc in each stitch.
Row 23: Turn, ch1, 2sc in next stitch, sc9, 2sc in last stitch (13 sts).
Rows 24–25: Turn, ch1, sc in each stitch.
Row 26: Turn, sc dec, sc9, sc dec (11 sts).
Rows 27–29: Turn, ch1, sc in each stitch.
Row 30: Turn, sc dec, sc7, sc dec (9 sts).
Row 31: Turn, ch1, sc in each stitch.
Row 32: Turn, sc dec, sc5, sc dec (7 sts).
Row 33: Turn, ch1, sc in each stitch.
Row 34: Turn, sc dec, sc3, sc dec (5 sts).
Row 35: Turn, ch1, sc in each stitch.
Fasten off. Weave in ends.

Side Panel (make 4)
Ch5.
Row 1: Sc in second chain from hook and in each chain across (4 sts).
Rows 2–85: Turn, ch1, sc in each stitch.
Fasten off, leaving a long tail.

Top Flap (make 2)
Ch4.
Row 1: Sc in second chain from hook and in each chain across (3 sts).
Row 2: Turn, ch1, 2sc in next stitch, sc, 2sc in last stitch (5 sts).
Row 3: Turn, ch1, 2sc in next stitch, sc3, 2sc in last stitch (7 sts).
Row 4: Turn, ch1, 2sc in next stitch, sc5, 2sc in last stitch (9 sts).
Row 5: Turn, ch1, 2sc in next stitch, sc7, 2sc in last stitch (11 sts).
Rows 6–15: Turn, ch1, sc in each stitch.
Row 16: Turn, ch1, sc in back loop only of each stitch.
Row 17: Turn, sc in each stitch.
Fasten off. Weave in ends.

Medium
Sole (make 4)
Ch6.
Row 1: Sc in second chain from hook and in each chain across (5 sts).
Row 2: Turn, ch1, 2sc in next stitch, sc3, 2sc in last stitch (7 sts).
Row 3: Turn, ch1, 2sc in next stitch, sc5, 2sc in last stitch (9 sts).
Row 4: Turn, ch1, 2sc in next stitch, sc7, 2sc in last stitch (11 sts).
Rows 5–13: Turn, ch1, sc in each stitch.
Row 14: Turn, sc dec, sc7, sc dec (9 sts).
Row 15: Turn, ch1, sc9.
Row 16: Turn, ch1, 2sc in next stitch, sc7, 2sc in last stitch (11 sts).
Rows 17–21: Turn, ch1, sc in each stitch.
Row 22: Turn, ch1, 2sc in next stitch, sc9, 2sc in last stitch (13 sts).
Rows 23–28: Turn, ch1, sc in each stitch.
Row 29: Turn, ch1, 2sc in next stitch, sc11, 2sc in last stitch (15 sts).
Rows 30–31: Turn, ch1, sc in each stitch.
Row 32: Turn, sc dec, sc11, sc dec (13 sts).
Rows 33–34: Turn, ch1, sc in each stitch.
Row 35: Turn, sc dec, sc9, sc dec (11 sts).
Row 36: Turn, ch1, sc in each stitch.
Row 37: Turn, sc dec, sc7, sc dec (9 sts).
Row 38: Turn, ch1, sc in each stitch.
Row 39: Turn, sc dec, sc5, sc dec (7 sts).
Row 40: Turn, ch1, sc in each stitch.
Row 41: Turn, sc dec, sc3, sc dec (5 sts).
Fasten off. Weave in ends.

Side Panel (make 4)
Ch5.
Row 1: Sc in second chain from hook and in each chain across (4 sts).
Rows 2–90: Turn, ch1, sc in each stitch.
Fasten off, leaving a long tail.

Top Flap (make 2)
Ch4.
Row 1: Sc in second chain from hook and in each chain across (3 sts).
Row 2: Turn, ch1, 2sc in next stitch, sc, 2sc in last stitch (5 sts).
Row 3: Turn, ch1, 2sc in next stitch, sc3, 2sc in last stitch (7 sts).
Row 4: Turn, ch1, 2sc in next stitch, sc5, 2sc in last stitch (9 sts).
Row 5: Turn, ch1, 2sc in next stitch, sc7, 2sc in last stitch (11 sts).
Rows 6–17: Turn, ch1, sc in each stitch.
Row 18: Turn, ch1, sc in back loop only of each stitch.
Row 19: Turn, sc in each stitch.
Fasten off. Weave in ends.

Large
Sole (make 4)
Ch6.
Row 1: Sc in second chain from hook and in each chain across (5 sts).
Row 2: Turn, ch1, 2sc in next stitch, sc3, 2sc in last stitch (7 sts).
Row 3: Turn, ch1, 2sc in next stitch, sc5, 2sc in last stitch (9 sts).
Row 4: Turn, ch1, 2sc in next stitch, sc7, 2sc in last stitch (11 sts).
Rows 5–15: Turn, ch1, sc in each stitch.
Row 16: Turn, sc dec, sc7, sc dec (9 sts).
Row 17: Turn, ch1, sc in each stitch.
Row 18: Turn, ch1, 2sc in next stitch, sc7, 2sc in last stitch (11 sts).
Rows 19–23: Turn, ch1, sc in each stitch.
Row 24: Turn, ch1, 2sc in next stitch, sc9, 2sc in last stitch (13 sts).
Rows 25–31: Turn, ch1, sc in each stitch.
Row 32: Turn, ch1, 2sc in next stitch, sc11, 2sc in last stitch (15 sts).
Rows 33–34: Turn, ch1, sc in each stitch.
Row 35: Turn, sc dec, sc11, sc dec (13 sts).
Rows 36–38: Turn, ch1, sc in each stitch.
Row 39: Turn, sc dec, sc9, sc dec (11 sts).
Row 40: Turn, ch1, sc in each stitch.
Row 41: Turn, sc dec, sc7, sc dec (9 sts).
Row 42: Turn, ch1, sc in each stitch.
Row 43: Turn, sc dec, sc5, sc dec (7 sts).
Row 44: Turn, ch1, sc in each stitch.
Row 45: Turn, sc dec, sc3, sc dec (5 sts).
Fasten off. Weave in ends.

Side Panel (make 4)

Ch5.

Row 1: Sc in second chain from hook and in each chain across (4 sts).

Rows 2–95: Turn, ch1, sc in each stitch.

Fasten off, leaving a long tail.

Top Flap (make 2)

Ch4.

Row 1: Sc in second chain from hook and in each chain across (3 sts).

Row 2: Turn, ch1, 2sc in next stitch, sc, 2sc in last stitch (5 sts).

Row 3: Turn, ch1, 2sc in next stitch, sc3, 2sc in last stitch (7 sts).

Row 4: Turn, ch1, 2sc in next stitch, sc5, 2sc in last stitch (9 sts).

Row 5: Turn, ch1, 2sc in next stitch, sc7, 2sc in last stitch (11 sts).

Rows 6–19: Turn, ch1, sc in each stitch.

Row 20: Turn, ch1, sc in back loop only of each stitch.

Row 21: Turn, sc in each stitch.

Fasten off. Weave in ends.

Finishing for All Sizes

Using yarn needle, sew two soles together for each loafer.

Using stitch markers, line the side panels evenly with the sole on each side. Sew together.

Last, use stitch markers to hold top flap in place at the toe end of loafer. Sew into place.

These are perfect for those who love all things sweet and dainty. They're adorned with just a bit of lace trim and a few beads that are sewn on after the slippers are finished. They add a special dress-up touch to those sweet little feet!

Finished Measurements
Children's Small: 5"/12.75 cm long, 2"/5 cm wide
Children's Medium: 6"/15.25 cm long, 2"/5 cm wide
Children's Large: 7"/17.75 cm long, 2.5"/6 cm wide

Yarn
- Red Heart Anne Geddes Baby, light worsted weight #3 yarn, 80% acrylic/20% nylon (310 yd/340 m, 3.5 oz/100 g per skein)
  1 skein #0301 Teddy

Hook and Other Materials
- E-4/3.5 mm crochet hook or size to obtain gauge
- Lace trim (.3 yd/.3 m)
- Pins
- Sewing needle and matching thread
- 14 small faux pearl beads

Gauge
20 sts and 20 rows in sc = 4"/10 cm square

Notes
- The slippers are worked in joined rounds from the center of the sole out.
- For a tutorial on Double Crochet Decrease (dc dec), see page 90.

Small (make 2)
Ch18.
Rnd 1: Turn, sc in second chain from hook, sc4, hdc3, dc8, 8dc in last chain, continue working on opposite side of chain, dc8, hdc3, sc5, sl st to first stitch to join rnd (40 sts).
Rnd 2: Ch1, 2sc in same stitch, hdc3, dc12, 2dc in next 8 stitches, dc12, hdc3, sl st to first stitch to join rnd (50 sts).
Rnd 3: Ch1, sc in same stitch, 2sc in next stitch, sc7, hdc8, (hdc, 2hdc in next stitch) 8 times, hdc8, sc7, 2sc in next stitch, sc, sl st to first stitch to join rnd (60 sts).
Rnd 4: Ch1, working in back loop only, sc18, hdc24, sc18, sl st to first stitch to join rnd.
Rnd 5: Ch1, sc18, (dc, dc dec) 8 times, sc18, sl st to first stitch to join rnd (52 sts).
Rnd 6: Ch1, sc18, dc dec 8 times, sc18, sl st to first stitch to join rnd (44 sts).
Rnd 7: Ch1, sc18, dc dec 4 times, sc18, sl st to first stitch to join rnd (40 sts).
Rnd 8: Ch1, sc18, dc dec 2 times, sc18, sl st to first stitch to join rnd (38 sts).
Fasten off. Weave in ends.

Medium (make 2)
Ch22.
Rnd 1: Turn, sc in second chain from hook, sc5, hdc4, dc10, 8dc in last chain, continue working on opposite side of chain, dc10, hdc4, sc6, sl st to first stitch to join rnd (48 sts).
Rnd 2: Ch1, 2sc in same stitch, hdc4, dc15, 2dc in next 8 stitches, dc15, hdc4, sl st to first stitch to join rnd (58 sts).
Rnd 3: Ch1, sc in same stitch, 2sc in next stitch, sc9, hdc10, (hdc, 2hdc in next stitch) 8 times, hdc10, sc9, 2sc in next stitch, sc, sl st to first stitch to join rnd (68 sts).
Rnd 4: Ch1, working in back loop only sc22, hdc24, sc22, sl st to first stitch to join rnd.
Rnd 5: Ch1, sc22, (c, dc dec) 8 times, sc18, sl st to first stitch to join rnd (60 sts).
Rnd 6: Ch1, sc22, dc dec 8 times, sc22, sl st to first stitch to join rnd (52 sts).
Rnd 7: Ch1, sc22, dc dec 4 times, sc22, sl st to first stitch to join rnd (48 sts).
Rnd 8: Ch1, sc22, dc dec 2 times, sc22, sl st to first stitch to join rnd (46 sts).
Fasten off. Weave in ends.

Large (make 2)

Ch26.

Rnd 1: Turn, sc in second chain from hook, sc7, hdc5, dc11, 8dc in last chain, continue working on opposite side of chain, dc11, hdc5, sc8, sl st to first stitch to join rnd (56 sts).

Rnd 2: Ch1, 2sc in same stitch, hdc6, dc17, 2dc in next 8 stitches, dc17, hdc6, sl st to first stitch to join rnd (66 sts).

Rnd 3: Ch1, sc in same stitch, 2sc in next stitch, sc11, hdc12, (hdc, 2hdc in next stitch) 8 times, hdc12, sc11, 2sc in next stitch, sc, sl st to first stitch to join rnd (76 sts).

Rnd 4: Ch1, working in back loop only sc26, hdc24, sc 26, sl st to first stitch to join rnd.

Rnd 5: Ch1, sc26, (dc, dc dec) 8 times, sc26, sl st to first stitch to join rnd (68 sts).

Rnd 6: Ch1, sc26, dc dec 8 times, sc26, sl st to first stitch to join rnd (60 sts).

Rnd 7: Ch1, sc26, dc dec 4 times, sc26, sl st to first stitch to join rnd (56 sts).

Rnd 8: Ch1, sc26, dc dec 2 times, sc26, sl st to first stitch to join rnd (54 sts).

Fasten off. Weave in ends.

Finishing for All Sizes

Measure the length of the opening for the foot in the slipper. Cut 2 lengths of lace trim just a tiny bit longer than that. For each slipper, pin the lace around the opening, starting at the back of the slipper. Using sewing needle and thread, sew the lace around the opening. Finish by adding 7 beads to the front of each slipper, using the needle and thread to sew them in place.

Your feet will thank you for the cute comfort these sandals bring.

Finished Measurements
Women's Small: 8"/20.5 cm long, 3.5"/8.9 cm wide
Women's Medium: 9"/23 cm long, 4"/10 cm wide
Women's Large: 10"/25.5 cm long, 4"/10 cm wide

Yarn
- I Love This Cotton!, medium worsted weight #4 yarn, 100% cotton (180 yd/164.5 m, 3.5 oz/100 g per skein)
  1 skein #40 Sage (Color A)
  1 skein #24 Ivory (Color B)

Hook and Other Materials
- US F-5/3.75 mm crochet hook or size to obtain gauge
- 2 brown medium buttons
- Coordinating sewing thread and needle
- Yarn needle

Gauge
16 sts and 16 rows in sc = 4"/10 cm square

Notes
- The soles are worked in joined rounds from the center out. Two soles are crocheted for each sandal (one in each color yarn), then sewn together.
- The toe strap is made separately and the foot strap is crocheted directly onto the toe strap. The back of the sandal is crocheted onto the sole, then the right and left ankle straps are crocheted onto the back of the sandal. Finally, the flowers are made and sewn on along with the buttons.
- Ch1 at beginning of rounds on soles does not count as a stitch.
- For a tutorial on Double Crochet Decrease (dc dec), see page 90.

Using Color A to sew the two soles together creates a decorative border around the upper portion of the sole.

Small
Sole (make 4)
NOTE: Make two in Color A and two in Color B.
Ch23.
Rnd 1: Turn, sc in second chain from hook, sc12, hdc5, dc3, 6dc in last stitch, continue working on opposite side of chain dc3, hdc5, sc13, sl st to first stitch to join rnd (48 sts).
Rnd 2: Ch2 (counts as first stitch), hdc in same stitch, hdc12, dc8, 2dc in next 6 stitches, dc8, hdc13, 2hdc in last stitch, sl st to first ch2 to join (56 sts).
Rnd 3: Ch1, sc in same stitch, 2sc in next stitch, sc7, sl st in next 3 stitches, hdc10, (hdc, 2hdc in next stitch) 6 times, hdc10, sl st in the next 3 stitches, sc8, 2sc in last stitch, sl st to first stitch (not the ch1) to join rnd (64 sts).
Rnd 4: Ch1, sc2, 2sc in next stitch, sc10, hdc16, (hdc2, 2hdc) two times, hdc16, sc11, 2sc in last stitch, sl st to first stitch to join (67 sts).
Rnd 5: Ch1, sc32, 2sc in next stitch, sc3, 2sc in next stitch, sc30, sl st to first stitch to join rnd (69 sts).
Fasten off, leaving a long tail. Weave in ends.
Using yarn needle and Color A, sew one sole of Color A and Color B together. Repeat for the other sole.

Toe Strap (make 2)
Using Color A, ch6.
Row 1: Turn, sc5 (5 sts).
Row 2: Ch1, sl st 5.
Rows 3–18: Repeat Rows 1 and 2.
Fasten off. Weave in ends.

Foot Strap
Row 1: Join Color A in the side of toe strap at Row 10, ch1, sc4 (4 sts).
Row 2: Turn, ch1, sl st 4.
Row 3: Turn, ch1, sc4.
Rows 4–21: Repeat Rows 2 and 3.
Repeat with other toe strap.

Back of Sandal
Locate the back center stitch of the sole. With the back of the sole facing you and the green side of the sole facing down, count 15 stitches to the right of that center stitch. Using Color A, join yarn in that stitch.
Row 1: Ch1, using back loop only of the top of the sole, sc26 around the back of the sole.
Row 2: Turn, ch1, sl st in each stitch.
Row 3: Turn, ch1, sc in each stitch.
Rows 4–11: Repeat Rows 2 and 3.
Fasten off. Weave in ends.
Repeat with other sandal.

Right Ankle Strap
Row 1: Using Color A, join yarn at the left edge of the back of the sandal at the end of Row 8, ch1, sc4 (4 sts).
Row 2: Turn, ch1, sl st 4.
Row 3: Turn, ch1, sc4.
Rows 4–15: Repeat Rows 2 and 3.
Row 16: Turn, ch1, sl st 4.
Row 17: Turn, ch1, sc1, ch3, skip 2 stitches, sc in last stitch.
Row 18: Turn, ch1, sl st, sl st 2 in ch3 space, sl st in last stitch.
Row 19: Turn, ch1, sc in each stitch.
Fasten off. Weave in ends.
Repeat with other sandal.

Left Ankle Strap
Row 1: Using Color A, join yarn at the right edge of the back of the sandal at the end of Row 11, ch1, sc4 (4 sts).
Row 2: Turn, ch1, sl st 4.
Row 3: Turn, ch1, sc4.
Rows 4–15: Repeat Rows 2 and 3.
Row 16: Turn, ch1, sl st 4.
Row 17: Turn, ch1, sc1, ch3, skip 2 stitches, sc in last stitch.
Row 18: Turn, ch1, sl st, sl st 2 in ch3 space, sl st in last stitch.
Row 19: Turn, ch1, sc in each stitch.
Fasten off. Weave in ends.
Repeat with other sandal.

Attaching Toe Strap
Locate the center stitch at the front of the sandal on each sole. Count 29 stitches to the left of that stitch and, using yarn needle and Color A, sew one end of the toe strap on. Count 29 stitches to the right of the center stitch and sew the other end of the toe strap to the sole.
Repeat with the other toe strap and sandal.

Medium
Sole (make 4)
NOTE: Make two in Color A and two in Color B.
Ch26.
Rnd 1: Turn, sc in second chain from hook, sc15, hdc5, dc3, 6dc in last stitch, continue working on opposite side of chain dc3, hdc5, sc16, sl st to first stitch to join rnd (54 sts).
Rnd 2: Ch2 (counts as first stitch), hdc in same stitch, hdc15, dc8, 2dc in next 6 stitches, dc8, hdc15, 2hdc in last stitch, sl st to first ch2 to join rnd (62 sts).
Rnd 3: Ch1, sc in same stitch, 2sc in next stitch, sc8, sl st in next 3 stitches, hdc12, (hdc, 2hdc in next stitch) 6 times, hdc12, sl st in next 3 stitches, sc9, 2sc in last stitch, sl st to first stitch (not the ch1) to join rnd (70 sts).
Rnd 4: Ch1, sc2, 2sc in next stitch, sc11, hdc18, (hdc2, 2hdc in next stitch) 2 times, hdc18, sc13, 2sc in last stitch, sl st to first stitch to join rnd (74 sts).
Rnd 5: Ch1, sc36, 2sc in next stitch, sc3, 2sc in next stitch, sc33, sl st to first stitch to join rnd (76 sts).
Fasten off, leaving a long tail. Weave in ends.
Using yarn needle and Color A, sew one sole of Color A and Color B together. Repeat for the other sole.

Toe Strap (make 2)
Using Color A, ch6.
Row 1: Turn, sc5 (5 sts).
Row 2: Ch1, sl st 5.
Rows 3–20: Repeat Rows 1 and 2.
Fasten off. Weave in ends.

Foot Strap
Row 1: Join Color A in the side of toe strap at Row 12, ch1, sc4 (4 sts).
Row 2: Turn, ch1, sl st 4.
Row 3: Turn, ch1, sc4.
Rows 4–19: Repeat Rows 2 and 3.
Fasten off. Weave in ends.
Repeat with other toe strap.

Back of Sandal
Locate the back center stitch of the sole. With the back of the sole facing you and the green side of the sole facing down, count 15 stitches to the right of that center stitch. Using Color A, join yarn in that stitch.
Row 1: Ch1, using back loop only of the top of the sole, sc28 around the sole (28 sts).
Row 2: Turn, ch1, sl st in each stitch.
Row 3: Turn, ch1, sc in each stitch.
Rows 4–11: Repeat Rows 2 and 3.
Fasten off. Weave in ends.
Repeat with other sandal.

Right Ankle Strap
Row 1: Using Color A, join yarn at the left edge of the back of the sandal at the end of Row 8, ch1, sc4 (4 sts).
Row 2: Turn, ch1, sl st 4.
Row 3: Turn, ch1, sc4.
Rows 4–17: Repeat Rows 2 and 3.
Row 18: Turn, ch1, sl st 4.
Row 19: Turn, ch1, sc1, ch3, skip 2 stitches, sc in last stitch.
Row 20: Turn, ch1, sl st, sl st 2 in ch3 space, sl st in last stitch.
Row 21: Turn, ch1, sc in each stitch.
Fasten off. Weave in ends.
Repeat with other sandal.

Left Ankle Strap
Row 1: Using Color A, join yarn at the right edge of the back of the sandal at Row 11, ch1, sc4 (4 sts).
Row 2: Turn, ch1, sl st 4.
Row 3: Turn, ch1, sc4.
Rows 4–17: Repeat Rows 2 and 3.
Row 18: Turn, ch1, sl st 4.
Row 19: Turn, ch1, sc1, ch3, skip 2 stitches, sc in last stitch.
Row 20: Turn, ch1, sl st, sl st 2 in ch3 space, sl st in last stitch.
Row 21: Turn, ch1, sc in each stitch.
Fasten off. Weave in ends.
Repeat with other sandal.

Attaching Toe Strap
Locate the center stitch at the front of the sandal on each sole. Count 31 stitches to the left of that stitch and, using yarn needle and Color A, sew one end of the toe strap on. Count 31 stitches to the right of the center stitch and sew the other end of the toe strap to the sole.
Repeat with other toe strap and sandal.

Large
Sole (make 4)
NOTE: Make two in Color A and two in Color B.
Ch29.
Rnd 1: Turn, sc in second chain from hook, sc18, hdc5, dc3, 6dc in last stitch, continue working on opposite side of chain dc3, hdc5, sc19, sl st to first stitch to join rnd (60 sts).
Rnd 2: Ch2 (counts as first stitch), hdc in same stitch, hdc19, dc8, 2dc in next 6 stitches, dc8, hdc18, 2hdc in last stitch, sl st to first ch2 to join rnd (68 sts).
Rnd 3: Ch1, sc in same stitch, 2sc in next stitch, sc8, sl st in next 3 stitches, hdc14, (hdc, 2hdc in next stitch) 6 times, hdc14, sl st in the next 3 stitches, sc11, 2sc in last stitch, sl st to first stitch (not the ch1) to join rnd (76 sts).
Rnd 4: Ch1, sc2, 2sc in next stitch, sc12, hdc20, (hdc2, 2hdc in next stitch) 2 times, hdc20, sc14, 2sc in last stitch, sl st to first stitch to join rnd (80 sts).
Rnd 5: Ch1, sc40, 2sc in next stitch, sc3, 2sc in next stitch, sc35, sl st to first stitch to join rnd (82 sts).
Fasten off, leaving a long tail. Weave in ends.
Using yarn needle and Color A, sew one sole of Color A and Color B together. Repeat for the other sole.

Toe Strap (make 2)
Using Color A, ch6.
Row 1: Turn, sc5.
Row 2: Ch1, sl st 5.
Rows 3–22: Repeat Rows 1 and 2.
Fasten off. Weave in ends.

Foot Strap
Row 1: Join Color A at the side of toe strap in Row 13, ch1, sc4 (4 sts).
Row 2: Turn, ch1, sl st 4.
Row 3: Turn, ch1, sc4.
Rows 4–21: Repeat Rows 2 and 3.
Fasten off. Weave in ends.
Repeat with other toe strap.

Back of Sandal

Locate the back center stitch of the sole. With the back of the sole facing you and the green side of the sole facing down, count 15 stitches to the right of that center stitch. Using Color A, join yarn in that stitch.

Row 1: Ch1, using back loop only of top of the sole, sc30 around the sole (30 sts).

Row 2: Turn, ch1, sl st in each stitch.

Row 3: Turn, ch1, sc in each stitch.

Rows 4–11: Repeat Rows 2–3.

Fasten off. Weave in ends.

Repeat with other sole.

Right Ankle Strap

Row 1: Using Color A, join yarn at left edge of back of sandal at end of Row 8, ch1, sc4.

Row 2: Turn, ch1, sl st 4.

Row 3: Turn, ch1, sc4.

Rows 4–21: Repeat Rows 2 and 3.

Row 22: Turn, ch1, sl st 4.

Row 23: Turn, ch1, sc1, ch3, skip 2 stitches, sc in last stitch.

Row 24: Turn, ch1, sl st, sl st 2 in ch3 space, sl st in last stitch.

Row 25: Turn, ch1, sc in each stitch.

Fasten off. Weave in ends.

Repeat with other sandal.

Left Ankle Strap

Row 1: Using Color A, join yarn at right edge of back of sandal at end of Row 11, ch1, sc4 (4 sts).

Row 2: Turn, ch1, sl st 4.

Row 3: Turn, ch1, sc4.

Rows 4–21: Repeat Rows 2 and 3.

Row 22: Turn, ch1, sl st 4.

Row 23: Turn, ch1, sc1, ch3, skip 2 stitches, sc in last stitch.

Row 24: Turn, ch1, sl st, sl st 2 in ch3 space, sl st in last stitch.

Row 25: Turn, ch1, sc in each stitch.

Fasten off. Weave in ends.

Repeat with other sandal.

Attaching Toe Strap

Locate the center stitch at the front of the sandal on each sole. Count 33 stitches to the left of that stitch and, using yarn needle and Color A, sew one end of the toe strap on. Count 33 stitches to the right of the center stitch and sew the other end of the toe strap to the sole.

Repeat with the other toe strap and sole.

Finishing for All Sizes

Fold foot strap down 14 rows and, with yarn needle and thread, sew the end to the back side of foot strap.

Slide ankle strap through the opening. Position a button as seen in the photo (right) and sew to attach it and the ankle strap to the back of the sandal.

Repeat with the other sandal.

Flower (make 2)

Using Color B, ch41.

Row 1: Turn, sc in each stitch (40 sts).

Row 2: Turn, ch1, *sc, tr in next stitch, repeat from * to complete row.

Fasten off, leaving a long tail.

Roll into a small rosette and, using yarn needle, secure the rosette so it won't come undone. Then attach rosette to sandal where the toe and foot strap join.

Fasten off. Weave in ends.

Repeat with other flower and sandal.

Placement of the button

Skill Level: Intermediate

Shaggy Boots

36

If these slipper boots don't make you run for your hook, then Houston, we have a problem! Your friends and family will be raving about how darling they are, and how clever you are! Just by mixing in a fun eyelash yarn, you can create something unique.

Finished Measurements

Children's Small: 6"/15.25 cm long, 2"/5 cm wide

Children's Medium: 7"/17.75 cm long, 2.5"/6 cm wide

Children's Large: 8"/20.25 cm long, 2.5"/6 cm wide

Yarn

- Baby Bee Hushabye Solid, medium worsted weight #4 yarn, 50% cotton/50% acrylic (208 yd/190 m; 3.5 oz/100 g per skein)
  1 skein #11 Naked (Color A)
- Lion Brand Romance Yarn, super bulky weight #6 yarn, 84% nylon/16% polyester (27 yd/25 m, 1.75 oz/50 g per skein)
  2 skeins #325-189 Merlot (Color B)

Hook and Other Materials

- US F-5/3.75 mm crochet hook or size to obtain gauge
- Yarn needle
- Small buckle to adjust strap on side

Gauge

16 sts and 12 rows in hdc = 4"/10 cm square

Notes

- The boot is worked out from the center of the sole up to the cuff.
- Color A and B are worked together for the cuff.
- For tutorials on Double Crochet Decrease (dc dec) and Half Double Crochet Decrease (hdc dec), see pages 90 and 88.

Small (make 2)

Using Color A, ch18.

Rnd 1: Turn, sc in second chain from hook, sc6, hdc5, dc4, 8dc in last chain, working continuously onto opposite side of chain, dc4, hdc5, sc7, sl st to first stitch to join rnd (40 sts).

Rnd 2: Ch1, 2sc in same stitch, sc3, hdc8, dc4, 2dc in next 8 stitches, dc4, hdc8, sc3, 2sc in last stitch, sl st to first stitch to join rnd (50 sts).

Rnd 3: Ch1, 2sc in same stitch, 2sc in next stitch, sc3, hdc9, dc3, (hdc, 2hdc in next stitch) 8 times, dc3, hdc9, sc4, 2sc in next 2 stitches, sc in last stitch, sl st to first stitch to join rnd (62 sts).

Rnd 4: Ch2 (does not count as a stitch here and throughout), working in back loop only, hdc in same stitch, hdc18, dc24, hdc19, sl st to first stitch to join rnd (62 sts).

Rnd 5: Ch2, hdc in same stitch, hdc18, (dc2, dc dec) 6 times, dc19, sl st to first stitch to join rnd (56 sts).

Rnd 6: Ch2, hdc in same stitch, hdc18, (dc, dc dec) 6 times, dc19, sl st to first stitch to join rnd (50 sts).

Rnd 7: Ch2, hdc in same stitch, hdc18, dc dec 6 times, hdc19, sl st to first stitch to join rnd (44 sts).

Rnd 8: Ch2 hdc in same stitch, hdc16, dc dec 5 times, hdc17, sl st to first stitch to join rnd (39 sts).

Join Color B.

Rnds 9–15: With Color A and B, ch2, dc in each stitch, sl st to first stitch to join rnd.

Fasten off. Weave in ends.

Medium (make 2)

Using Color A, ch22.

Rnd 1: Turn, sc in second chain from hook, sc8, hdc6, dc5, 8dc in last chain, working continuously onto opposite side of chain, dc5, hdc6, sc9, sl st to first stitch to join rnd (48 sts).

Rnd 2: Ch1, 2sc in same stitch, sc5, hdc10, dc4, 2dc in next 8 stitches, dc4, hdc10, sc5, 2sc in last stitch, sl st to first stitch to join rnd (58 sts).

Rnd 3: Ch1, 2sc in same stitch, 2sc in next stitch, sc3, hdc13, dc3, (hdc, 2hdc in next stitch) 8 times, dc3, hdc13, sc4, 2sc in next 2 stitches, sl st to first stitch to join rnd (70 sts).

Rnd 4: Ch2 (does not count as a stitch here and throughout), working in back loop only, hdc in same stitch, hdc22, dc24, hdc23, sl st to first stitch to join rnd.

Rnd 5: Ch2, hdc23, (dc2, dc dec) 6 times, hdc23, sl st to first stitch to join rnd (62 sts).

Rnd 6: Ch2, hdc in same stitch, hdc22, (dc, dc dec) 8 times, hdc23, sl st to first stitch to join rnd (54 sts).

Rnd 7: Ch2, hdc in same stitch, hdc17, dc dec 11 times, hdc18, sl st to first stitch to join rnd (43 sts).

Rnd 8: Ch2, hdc in same stitch, hdc17, dc dec 2 times, dc dec 3 together, dc dec 2 times, hdc18, sl st to first stitch to join rnd (37 sts).

Rnd 9: Ch2, hdc in same stitch, hdc13 dc dec 2 times, dc, dc dec 2 times, hdc14, sl st to first stitch to join rnd (33 sts).

Join Color B.

Rnds 10–15: With Color A and B, ch2, dc in each stitch, sl st to first stitch to join rnd.

Fasten off. Weave in ends.

Large (make 2)

Using Color A, ch 26.

Rnd 1: Turn, sc in second chain from hook, sc10, hdc7, dc6, 8dc in last chain, working continuously onto opposite side of chain, dc6, hdc7, sc11, sl st to first stitch to join rnd (56 sts).

Rnd 2: Ch1, 2sc in same stitch, sc5, hdc13, dc5, 2dc in next 8 stitches, dc5, hdc13, sc5, 2sc in last stitch, sl st to first stitch to join rnd (66 sts).

Rnd 3: Ch1, 2sc in same stitch, 2sc in next stitch, sc3, hdc16, dc4, (hdc, 2hdc in next stitch) 8 times, dc4, hdc16, sc3, 2sc in next 2 stitches, sl st to first stitch to join rnd (78 sts).

Rnd 4: Ch2 (does not count as a stitch here and throughout), working in back loop only, hdc in same stitch, hdc26, dc24, hdc27 sl st to first stitch to join rnd.

Rnd 5: Ch2, hdc in the same stitch, hdc26, (dc2, dc dec) 6 times, dc27, sl st to first stitch to join rnd (72 sts).

Rnd 6: Ch2, hdc in same stitch, hdc26, (dc, dc dec) 6 times, dc27, sl st to first stitch to join rnd (66 sts).

Rnd 7: Ch2, hdc in same stitch, hdc21, * dc dec 11 times, hdc22, sl st to first stitch to join rnd (55 sts).

Rnd 8: Ch2, hdc in same stitch, hdc21, dc dec 2 times, dc dec 3 together, dc dec 2 times, hdc22, sl st to first stitch to join rnd (49 sts).

Rnd 9: Ch2, hdc in same stitch, hdc19, dc dec 2 times, dc, dc dec 2 times, hdc20, sl st to first stitch to join rnd (45 sts).

Rnd 10: Ch2, hdc in same stitch, hdc17, hdc dec 2 times, hdc, hdc dec 2 times, hdc18, sl st to first stitch to join rnd (41 sts).

Join Color B.

Rnds 11–16: With Color A and B, ch2, dc in each stitch, sl st to first stitch to join rnd.

Fasten off. Weave in ends.

Adjusting Strap for All Sizes

Using Color A, ch61.

Row 1: Turn, sc in first chain from hook and in each across (60 sts).

Fasten off. Weave in ends.

Secure around fuzzy cuff with buckle.

Skill Level: Intermediate

Men's Goldenrod Slipper Socks

Make this simple slipper sock for the men in your life and help them relax after a hard day's work.

Finished Measurements

Men's Small: 9.5"/24.25 cm long, 4"/10 cm wide

Men's Medium: 10.5"/26.75 cm long, 4"/10 cm wide

Men's Large: 11.5"/29.25 cm long, 4"/10 cm wide

Yarn

- Lion Brand Heartland, medium worsted weight #4 yarn, 100% acrylic (251 yd/230 m, 5 oz/142 g per skein)
    1 skein #136-158 Yellowstone

Hook and Other Materials

- US H-8/5 mm crochet hook or size to obtain gauge
- Stitch marker
- Yarn needle

Gauge

16 sts and 16 rows in sc = 4"/10 cm square

Notes

- The slipper is worked from the toe up, first continuously in the round, then switching to rows for the heel, then in joined rounds to the end. The toe opening and heel then get sewn closed.
- Use a stitch marker to mark the beginning of each round.
- For a tutorial on Single Crochet Decrease (sc dec), see page 87.

Small (make 2)

Ch18, sl st to first chain to join.

Rnd 1: Ch1, sc in each chain (18 sts).

Rnd 2: Working continuously in the round, *sc2, 2sc in next stitch, repeat from * to complete rnd (24 sts).

Rnd 3: *Sc3, 2sc in next stitch, repeat from * to complete rnd (30 sts).

Rnd 4: *Sc4, 2sc in next stitch, repeat from * to complete rnd (36 sts).

Rnds 5–23: Sc in each stitch.

Rows 24–37: Turn, ch1, sc26 (26 sts).

Row 38: Turn, ch1, sc8, sc dec 5 times, sc8 (21 sts).

Rnd 39: Sl st to opposite corner of heel flap, turn, using ends of rows as stitches sc 14, sc10 across foot, sc14 on opposite side of heel, sl st to first stitch to join (42 sts).

Rnd 40: Ch1, sc14, sc dec, sc10, sc dec, sc14, sl st to first stitch to join (40 sts).

Rnds 41–43: Ch2 (do not count as a stitch), fpsc, *fpc2, bpsc in next stitch, repeat from * to complete rnd, sl st to first stitch to join.

Fasten off. Weave in ends.

Medium (make 2)

Ch18, sl st to first chain to join.

Rnd 1: Ch1, sc in each chain (18 sts).

Rnd 2: Working continuously in the round, *sc2, 2sc in next stitch, repeat from * to complete rnd (24 sts).

Rnd 3: *Sc3, 2sc in next stitch, repeat from * to complete the rnd (30 sts).

Rnd 4: *Sc4, 2sc in next stitch, repeat from * to complete the rnd (36 sts).

Rnds 5–26: Sc in each stitch.

Rows 27–41: Turn, ch1, sc26 (26 sts).

Row 42: Turn, ch1, sc8, sc dec 5 times, sc8 (21 sts).

Rnd 43: Sl st to opposite corner of heel, turn, using ends of rows as stitches, sc 14, sc10 across foot, sc14 on opposite side of heel, sl st to first stitch to join (42 sts).

Rnd 44: Ch1, sc14, sc dec, sc10, sc dec, sc14, sl st to first stitch to join (40 sts).

Rnds 45–47: Ch2 (does not count as a stitch), fpsc, *fpsc2, bpsc in next stitch, repeat from * to complete rnd, sl st to first stitch to join.

Fasten off. Weave in ends.

Large (make 2)

Ch20, sl st to first chain to join.

Rnd 1: Ch1, sc in each chain (20 sts).

Rnd 2: Working continuously in the round, *sc4, 2sc in next stitch, repeat from * to complete rnd (24 sts).

Rnd 3: *Sc5, 2sc in next stitch, repeat from * to complete rnd (28 sts).

Rnd 4: *Sc6, 2sc in next stitch, repeat from * to complete rnd (32 sts).

Rnd 5: *Sc7, 2sc in next stitch, repeat from * to complete rnd (36 sts).

Rnd 6: *Sc8, 2sc in next stitch, repeat from * to complete the rnd (40 sts).

Rnds 7–30: Sc in each stitch.

Rows 31–48: Turn, ch1, sc30 (30 sts).

Row 49: Turn, ch1, sc9, sc dec 6 times, sc9 (24 sts).

Rnd 50: Sl st to opposite corner of heel, turn, using ends of rows as stitches, sc17, sc10 across foot, sc17 on opposite side of heel, sl st to first stitch to join (44 sts).

Rnd 51: Ch1, sc15, sc dec, sc10, sc dec, sc15, sl st to first stitch to join (42 sts).

Rnds 52–54: Ch2 (do not count as a stitch), fpsc, *fpsc2, bpsc in next stitch, repeat from * to complete rnd, sl st to first stitch to join (42 sts).

Fasten off. Weave in ends.

Finishing for All Sizes

Use yarn needle to sew closed the toe and heel openings.

Skill Level: Intermediate

Frog Loafers

Let your little one hop around with excitement in these adorable loafers! If you want, add the eyes, or leave them off for a fun basic loafer for boys or girls.

Finished Measurements
Children's Small: 5.5"/14 cm long, 2"/5 cm wide
Children's Medium: 6.5"/16.5 cm long, 2"/5 cm wide
Children's Large: 7.5"/19 cm long, 2.5"/6.5 cm wide

Yarn
- Lion Brand Vanna's Choice, medium worsted weight #4 yarn, 100% acrylic (170 yd/156 m, 3.5 oz/100 g per skein)
    1 skein #860-171 Fern (Color A)
    1 skein #860-153 Black (Color B)
    1 skein #860-100 White (Color C)

Hook and Other Materials
- US F-5/3.75 mm crochet hook or size to obtain gauge
- Yarn needle

Gauge
16 sts and rows in sc = 4"/10 cm square

Notes
- The loafers are worked from the center of the sole out in joined rounds.
- The ch1 and sl st in each round do not count as a stitch.

Small (make 2)
Using Color A, ch17.
Rnd 1: Hdc in third chain from hook, hdc13, 6hdc in last chain, working continuously on opposite side of chain, hdc14, sl st to first stitch to join rnd (34 sts).
Rnd 2: Ch1, 2sc in same stitch, sc6, hdc3, dc4, 2dc in next 6 stitches, dc4, hdc3, sc6, 2sc in last stitch, sl st to first stitch to join rnd (42 sts).
Rnd 3: Ch1, sc in same stitch, 2sc in next stitch, hdc13, (hdc in next stitch, 2hdc in next stitch) 6 times, hdc13, 2sc in next stitch, sc in last stitch, sl st to first stitch to join rnd (50 sts).
Rnd 4: Turn, ch1, in back loop only for all stitches to end of rnd, sc in same stitch, sc15, hdc2, dc18, hdc2, sc16, sl st to first stitch to join rnd.
Rnd 5: Ch1, sc in same stitch, sc17, (dc, dc dec) 6 times, sc18, sl st to first stitch to join rnd (44 sts).
Rnd 6: Ch1, sc in same stitch, sc17, in back loops only sc dec 6 times, using both loops sc18, sl st to first stitch to join rnd (38 sts).
Rnd 7: Ch1, sc in same stitch, sc17, sc dec 3 times, sc18, sl st to first stitch to join rnd (35 sts).
Fasten off. Weave in ends.

Medium (make 2)
Using Color A, ch21.

Rnd 1: Hdc in third chain from hook, hdc17, 6hdc in last chain, working continuously on opposite side of chain, hdc18, sl st to first stitch to join rnd (42 sts).

Rnd 2: Ch1, 2sc in same stitch, sc6, hdc6, dc5, 2dc in next 6 stitches, dc5, hdc6, sc6, 2sc in last stitch, sl st to first stitch to join rnd (50 sts).

Rnd 3: Ch1, sc in same stitch, 2sc in next stitch, hdc17, (hdc in next stitch, 2hdc in next stitch) 6 times, hdc18, 2sc in next stitch, sc in last stitch, sl st to first stitch to join rnd (58 sts).

Rnd 4: Turn, ch1, in back loop only of all stitches to end of rnd, sc in same stitch, sc18, hdc2, dc18, hdc2, sc18, sl st to first stitch to join rnd (58 sts).

Rnd 5: Ch1, sc in same stitch, sc19, (dc, dc dec) 6 times, sc20, sl st to first stitch to join rnd (52 sts).

Rnd 6: Ch1, sc in same stitch, sc19, in back loops only sc dec 6 times, using both loops sc20, sl st to first stitch to join rnd (46 sts).

Rnd 7: Ch1, sc in same stitch, sc19, sc dec 3 times, sc20, sl st to first stitch to join rnd (43 sts).

Fasten off. Weave in ends.

Large (make 2)
Using Color A, ch25.

Rnd 1: Hdc in third chain from hook, hdc21, 6hdc in last chain, working continuously on opposite side of chain, hdc22, sl st to first stitch to join rnd (50 sts).

Rnd 2: Ch1, 2sc in same stitch, sc8, hdc6, dc7, 2dc in next 6 stitches, dc7, hdc6, sc8, 2sc in last stitch, sl st to first stitch to join rnd (58 sts).

Rnd 3: Ch1, sc in same stitch, 2sc in next stitch, hdc21, (hdc in next stitch, 2hdc in next stitch) 6 times, hdc21, 2sc in next stitch, sc in last stitch, sl st to first stitch to join rnd (66 sts).

Rnd 4: Turn, ch1, in back loop only of all stitches to end of rnd, sc in same stitch, sc22, hdc2, dc18, hdc2, sc22, sl st to first stitch to join rnd (66 sts).

Rnd 5: Ch1, sc in same stitch, sc23, (dc, dc dec) 6 times, sc24, sl st to first stitch to join rnd (60 sts).

Rnd 6: Ch1, sc in same stitch, sc23, in back loops only sc dec 6 times, using both loops sc24, sl st to first stitch to join rnd (54 sts).

Rnd 7: Ch1, sc in same stitch, sc23, sc dec 3 times, sc24, sl st to first stitch to join rnd (51 sts).

Fasten off. Weave in ends.

Straps for All Sizes
Right Loafer

On right side of loafer, locate the exposed loop on Rnd 6. Join Color A on Rnd 4 below that loop.

Row 1: Working toward the back of loafer, ch1, sc6.

Rows 2–13: Turn, ch1, sc6.

Row 14: Turn, sc dec, sc2, sc dec (4 sts).

Row 15: Turn, sc dec 2 times (2 sts).

Fasten off. Weave in ends.

Left Loafer

On left side of shoe, locate the exposed loop on Rnd 6. Count 6 stitches toward the heel, join Color A.

Row 1: Working toward the front of shoe, ch1, sc6.

Rows 2–13: Turn, ch1, sc6.

Row 14: Turn, sc dec, sc2, sc dec (4 sts).

Row 15: Turn, sc dec 2 times (2 sts).

Fasten off. Weave in ends.

Eyes (make 2; optional)
Using Color B, ch2.

Rnd 1: 5sc in first chain, sl st to first stitch.

Fasten off.

Rnd 2: Join Color C, ch2, 2dc in each stitch, sl st to first stitch (not ch2) to join rnd (10 sts).

Fasten off.

Rnd 3: Join Color A, ch1, * sc, 2sc, repeat from * to complete rnd, sl st to first stitch to join rnd.

Fasten off, leaving a 10"/25.5 cm tail.

Finishing for All Sizes
Using yarn needle, sew the edge of the eyes on the straps. Then, sew the edge of the strap onto opposite side of the loafer.

Fasten off. Weave in ends.

Skill Level: **Advanced**

Cabled Slipper Socks

45

***T**hese slipper socks are so cozy to snuggle into after a long day! The cable crossover is created by crocheting stitches out of order.*

Finished Measurements
Women's Small: 8"/20.5 cm long, 3.5"/8.9 cm wide
Women's Medium: 9"/23 cm long, 4"/10 cm wide
Women's Large: 10"/25.5 cm long, 4"/10 cm wide

Yarn
- I Love This Yarn!, medium worsted weight #4 yarn, 100% acrylic (355 yd/325 m, 7 oz/199 g per skein)
   1 skein #110 Turquoise (Color A)
   1 skein #352 Rouge (Color B)

Hook and Other Materials
- US F-5/3.75 mm crochet hook or size to obtain gauge
- Yarn needle

Gauge
16 sts and 16 rows in sc = 4"/10 cm square

Notes
- The slipper is worked from the cuff down to the toe in joined rounds, except for the heel to allow for give. The heel and toe seams are sewn together afterward.
- For the cable section, after joining the round, you will turn your work. This is done so that the stitches in the cable align properly.
- For tutorials on Front Post Double Crochet (fpdc), Back Post Double Crochet (bpdc), Front Post Treble Crochet (fptr), and Single Crochet Decrease (sc dec), see pages 94, 96, 97, and 87.

Small (make 2)
Using Color A, ch43.
Row 1: Turn, sc in second chain from hook and in each across (42 sts).
Row 2: Turn, ch3, dc in each stitch.
Row 3: Turn, Ch3, *fpdc2, bpdc, repeat from * to end of row, ending on fpdc2, sl st to ch3 to join, leaving a V in back.
Rnd 4: Ch3, *fpdc2, bpdc, repeat from * to end of row, ending on fpdc2, sl st to ch3 to join rnd.
Rnd 5: Ch1, sc in each stitch, sl st to ch1 to join rnd.
Join Color B, fasten off Color A.
Rnd 6: Ch1, sc in each stitch, sl st to ch1 to join rnd.
Rnd 7: Ch1, sc14, fpdc, sc, fpdc9, sc, fpdc, sc14, sl st to ch1 to join rnd.
Rnd 8: Turn, ch1, sc14, bpdc, sc, bpdc9, sc, fpdc, sc14, sl st to ch1 to join rnd.
Rnd 9: Turn, ch1, sc14, fpdc, sc, [fptr in each of the next 9 stitches, working them in this order: 1, 2, 3, 7, 9, 8, 3, 4, and 5], sc in next stitch, fpdc, sc14, sl st to ch1 to join rnd.
Rnd 10: Turn, ch1, sc14, bpdc, sc, bpdc9, sc, bpdc, sc14, sl st to ch1 to join rnd.
Rnd 11: Turn, ch1, sc14, fpdc, sc, over the next 9 stitches [fptr in stitches 4, 5, and 6, turn, bptr in stitches 1, 2, and 3, turn, and fptr in stitches 7, 8, and 9], sc in next stitch, fptr, sc14, sl st to first ch1 to join rnd.
Rnd 12: Repeat Rnd 10.
Rnd 13: Repeat Rnd 9.
Rnd 14: Repeat Rnd 10.
Rnd 15: Repeat Rnd 11.
Rnd 16: Repeat Rnd 10.
Rnd 17: Repeat Rnd 9.
Rnd 18: Repeat Rnd 10.
Rnd 19: Repeat Rnd 11.
Row 20: Turn, ch1, sc10 (10 sts).
Rows 21–29: Turn, ch1 sc20 (20 sts).
Rnd 30: Sl st to opposite corner of heel flap, sc9 on edge of flap, sc4, bpdc, sc, bpdc9, sc, bpdc, sc4, sc9 on opposite edge of flap, sl st to first stitch to join rnd.
Rnd 31: Turn, sc13, fpdc, sc, [fptr in each of the next 9 stitches in this order: 1, 2, 3, 7, 9, 8, 3, 4, and 5], sc in next stitch, fpdc, sc13 (39 sts).
Rnd 32: Turn, ch1, sc13, bpdc, sc, bpdc9, sc, bpdc, sc13.
Rnd 33: Turn, ch1, sc13, fpdc, sc, over the next 9 stitches [fptr in stitches 4, 5, and 6, turn, bptr in stitches 1, 2, and 3, turn, and fptr in stitches 7, 8, and 9], sc in next stitch, fptr, sc13, sl st to first ch1 to join rnd.
Rnd 34: Repeat Rnd 32.
Rnd 35: Repeat Rnd 31.
Rnd 36: Repeat Rnd 32.
Rnd 37: Repeat Rnd 33.
Rnd 38: Repeat Rnd 32.
Rnd 39: Repeat Rnd 31.
Rnd 40: Repeat Rnd 32.
Rnd 41: Repeat Rnd 33.
Rnd 42: Repeat Rnd 32.
Rnd 43: Repeat Rnd 31.
Rnd 44: Repeat Rnd 32.

Rnd 45: Repeat Rnd 33.
Rnd 46: Repeat Rnd 32.
Join Color A, fasten off Color B.
Rnds 47–49: Turn, ch1, sc in each stitch, sl st to ch1 to join rnd.
Rnd 50: Ch1, *sc11, sc dec, repeat from * 2 more times, sl st to ch1 to join rnd (36 sts).
Rnd 51: Ch1, * sc4, 2sc, repeat from * to complete rnd (30 sts).
Rnd 52: Ch1, * sc3, 2sc, repeat from * to complete rnd (24 sts).
Rnd 53: Ch1, * sc2, 2sc, repeat from * to complete rnd (18 sts).
Fasten off. Weave in ends.
Using yarn needle and Color B, sew heel opening together. Sew toe closed in line with heel.
Weave in ends.

Medium (make 2)

Using Color A, ch43.
Row 1: Turn, sc in second chain from hook and in each across (42 sts).
Row 2: Turn, ch3, dc in each stitch.
Row 3: Turn, ch3, *fpdc2, bpdc, repeat from * ending on fpdc2, sl st to ch3 to join, leaving a V in back.
Rnd 4: Ch3, *fpdc2, bpdc, repeat from * ending on fpdc2, sl st to ch3 to join rnd.
Rnd 5: Ch1, sc in each stitch, sl st to ch1 to join rnd.
Join Color B, fasten off Color A.
Rnd 6: Ch1, sc in each stitch, sl st to ch1 to join rnd.
Rnd 7: Ch1, sc14, fpdc, sc, fpdc9, sc, fpdc, sc14, sl st to ch1 to join rnd.
Rnd 8: Turn, ch1, sc14, bpdc, sc, bpdc9, sc, fpdc, sc14, sl st to ch1 to join rnd.
Rnd 9: Turn, ch1, sc14, fpdc, sc, [fptr in each of the next 9 stitches in this order: 1, 2, 3, 7, 9, 8, 3, 4, and 5], sc in next stitch, fpdc, sc14, sl st to ch1 to join rnd.
Rnd 10: Turn, ch1, sc14, bpdc, sc, bpdc9, sc, bpdc, sc14, sl st to ch1 to join rnd.
Rnd 11: Turn, ch1, sc14, fpdc, sc, over the next 9 stitches [fptr in stitches 4, 5, and 6, turn, bptr in stitches 1, 2, and 3, turn, fptr in stitches 7, 8, and 9], sc in next stitch, fptr, sc14, sl st to first ch1 to join rnd.
Rnd 12: Repeat Rnd 10.
Rnd 13: Repeat Rnd 9.
Rnd 14: Repeat Rnd 10.
Rnd 15: Repeat Rnd 11.
Rnd 16: Repeat Rnd 10.
Rnd 17: Repeat Rnd 9.
Rnd 18: Repeat Rnd 10.
Rnd 19: Repeat Rnd 11.
Row 20: Turn, ch1, sc10, sl st to ch1 to join rnd (10 sts).
Rows 21–29: Turn, ch1, sc20, sl st to ch1 to join rnd (20 sts).
Rnd 30: Sl st to opposite corner of heel flap, sc9 on edge of flap, sc4, bpdc, sc, bpdc9, sc, bpdc, sc4, sc9 on opposite edge of flap, sl st to first stitch to join.
Rnd 31: Turn, sc13, fpdc, sc, [fptr in each of the next 9 stitches in this order: 1, 2, 3, 7, 9, 8, 3, 4, and 5], sc in next stitch, fpdc, sc13, sl st to the first ch1 to join rnd (39 sts).
Rnd 32: Turn, ch1, sc13, bpdc, sc, bpdc9, sc, bpdc, sc13, sl st to the first ch1 to join rnd.
Rnd 33: Turn, ch1, sc13, fpdc, sc, over the next 9 stitches [fptr in stitches 4, 5, and 6, turn, bptr in stitches 1, 2, and 3, turn, fptr in stitches 7, 8, and 9], sc in next stitch, fptr, sc13, sl st to first ch1 to join rnd.
Rnd 34: Repeat Rnd 32.
Rnd 35: Repeat Rnd 31.
Rnd 36: Repeat Rnd 32.
Rnd 37: Repeat Rnd 33.
Rnd 38: Repeat Rnd 32.
Rnd 39: Repeat Rnd 31.
Rnd 40: Repeat Rnd 32.
Rnd 41: Repeat Rnd 33.
Rnd 42: Repeat Rnd 32.
Rnd 43: Repeat Rnd 31.
Rnd 44: Repeat Rnd 32.
Rnd 45: Repeat Rnd 33.
Rnd 46: Repeat Rnd 32.
Join Color A, fasten off Color B.
Rnds 47–49: Turn, ch1, sc in each stitch, sl st to ch1 to join rnd.
Rnd 50: Ch1, *sc11, sc dec, repeat from * 2 more times, sl st to ch1 to join rnd (36 sts).
Rnd 51: Ch1, *sc4, 2sc in next stitch, repeat from * to complete rnd, sl st to ch1 to join rnd (30 sts).
Rnd 52: Ch1, *sc3, 2sc in next stitch, repeat from * to complete rnd, sl st to ch1 to join rnd (24 sts).
Rnd 53: Ch1, *sc2, 2sc in next stitch, repeat from * to complete rnd, sl st to ch1 to join rnd (18 sts).
Fasten off. Weave in ends.
Using yarn needle and Color B, sew heel opening together. Sew toe closed in line with heel.
Weave in ends.

Large (make 2)

Using a US H-8/5.0 mm hook, follow the directions for Medium.

Skill Level: Intermediate

Striped Mary Jane Slippers

Whether you're crocheting this for yourself or a loved one, it is sure to be a hit. The stitches will keep your feet warm and your eyes intrigued.

Finished Measurements
Women's Small: 8"/20.5 cm long, 3.5"/8.9 cm wide
Women's Medium: 9"/23 cm long, 4"/10 cm wide
Women's Large: 10"/25.5 cm long, 4"/10 cm wide

Yarn
- Red Heart Soft, medium worsted weight #4 yarn, 100% acrylic (256 yd/234 m, 5 oz/141 g per skein)
    1 skein #9010 Charcoal (Color A)
    1 skein #9518 Teal (Color B)
    1 skein #3729 Grape (Color C)
    1 skein #9779 Berry (Color D)

Hook and Other Materials
- US E-4/3.5 mm crochet hook or size to obtain gauge
- Yarn needle

Gauge
18 sts and 20 rows in sc = 4"/10 cm square

Notes
- The slipper is worked in joined rounds from the center of the sole out.
- When switching between the different colors, you will carry the yarn you are not working with, not fasten it off. That will allow you to simply pick the yarn up later, with no ends to weave in. For a tutorial, see page 100.
- To change colors, push the hook through the next stitch, pull the yarn back through, yarn over with the *next* color, and pull through. Color change is complete. For a tutorial, see page 99.
- For tutorials on Double Crochet Decrease (dc dec), Front Post Double Crochet (fpdc), and Front Post Double Crochet Decrease (fpdc dec), see pages 90 and 94.

Small (make 2)

With Color A, ch21.

Rnd 1: Turn, sc in second chain from hook, sc5, sl st 3, sc4, hdc6, 6dc in last stitch, continue working on opposite side of chain, hdc6, sc4, sl st 3, sc6 sl st to first stitch to join rnd (44 sts).

Rnd 2: Ch1, 2sc in same stitch, sc8, hdc10, 2hdc in next 6 stitches, hdc10, sc8, 2sc in last stitch, sl st to first stitch to join rnd (52 sts).

Rnd 3: Ch1, sc in same stitch, 2sc in next stitch, sc8, hdc10, (hdc, 2hdc in next stitch) 6 times, hdc10, sc8, 2sc in next stitch, sc in last stitch sl st to first stitch to join rnd (60 sts).

Rnd 4: Ch1, sc in same stitch, sc, 2sc in next stitch, sc11, hdc6, (hdc2, 2hdc in next stitch) 6 times, hdc6, sc11, 2sc in next stitch, sc2, sl st to first stitch to join rnd (68 sts).

Rnd 5: Ch1, sc in same stitch, sc2, 2sc in next stitch, sc7, hdc10, (sc3, 2sc in next stitch) 6 times, hdc10, sc7, 2sc in next stitch, sc3, sl st to first stitch to join rnd (76 sts).

Rnd 6: Drop Color A, join Color B, ch 2, working in back loop only, fpdc23, (fpdc3, fpdc dec) 6 times, fpdc23, sl st to first stitch to join rnd (70 sts).

Rnd 7: Drop Color B, join Color C, ch2, fpdc23, (fpdc2, fpdc dec) 6 times, fpdc23, sl st to first stitch to join rnd (64 sts).

Rnd 8: Drop Color C, join Color D, ch2, fpdc23, (fpdc, fpdc dec) 6 times, fpdc23, sl st to first stitch to join rnd (58 sts).

Rnd 9: Drop Color D, pick up Color C, ch2, fpdc21, fpdc dec 8 times, fpdc21, sl st to first stitch to join rnd (50 sts).

Rnd 10: Drop Color C, pick up Color B, ch2, fpdc21, fpdc dec 4 times, fpdc21, sl st to first stitch to join rnd (46 sts).

Rnd 11: Drop Color B, pick up Color A, ch2, fpdc21, fpdc dec 2 times, fpdc21, sl st to first stitch to join rnd (44 sts).

Rnd 12: Ch1, sc18, ch7, sl st to stitch 34, turn, sl st in each chain, sl st to stitch 19, sc in each stitch to end of rnd.

Fasten off all colors. Weave in ends.

Medium (make 2)

With Color A, ch25.

Rnd 1: Turn, sc in second chain from hook, sc6, sl st 3, sc5, hdc8, 6dc in last stitch, continue working on opposite side of chain, hdc8, sc5, sl st 3, sc7 sl st to first stitch to join rnd (52 sts).

Rnd 2: Ch1, 2sc in same stitch, sc9, hdc13, 2hdc in next 6 stitches, hdc13, sc9, 2sc in last stitch, sl st to first stitch to join rnd (60 sts).

Rnd 3: Ch1, sc in same stitch, 2sc in next stitch, sc9, hdc13, (hdc, 2hdc in next stitch) 6 times, hdc13, sc9, 2sc in next stitch, sc in last stitch sl st to first stitch to join rnd (68 sts).

Rnd 4: Ch1, sc in same stitch, sc, 2sc in next stitch, sc15, hdc7, (hdc2, 2hdc in next stitch) 6 times, hdc7, sc15, 2sc in next stitch, sc2, sl st to first stitch to join rnd (76 sts).

Rnd 5: Ch1, sc in same stitch, sc2, 2sc in next stitch, sc10, hdc12, (sc3, 2sc in next stitch) 6 times, hdc12, sc10, 2sc in next stitch, sc3, sl st to first stitch to join rnd (84 sts).

Rnd 6: Drop Color A, join Color B, ch 2, working in back loop only, fpdc27, (fpdc3, fpdc dec) 6 times, fpdc27, sl st to first stitch to join rnd (78 sts).

Rnd 7: Drop Color B, join Color C, ch2, fpdc27, (fpdc2, fpdc dec) 6 times, fpdc27, sl st to first stitch to join rnd (72 sts).

Rnd 8: Drop Color C, join Color D, ch2, fpdc27, (fpdc, fpdc dec) 6 times, fpdc27, sl st to first stitch to join rnd (66 sts).

Rnd 9: Drop Color D, pick up Color C, ch2, fpdc25, fpdc dec 8 times, fpdc25, sl st to first stitch to join rnd (58 sts).

Rnd 10: Drop Color C, pick up Color B, ch2, fpdc25, fpdc dec 4 times, fpdc25, sl st to first stitch to join rnd (54 sts).

Rnd 11: Drop Color B, pick up Color A, ch2, fpdc25, fpdc dec 2 times, fpdc25, sl st to first stitch to join rnd (52 sts).

Rnd 12: Ch1, sc19, ch7, sl st to stitch 33, turn, sl st each chain, sl st to stitch 20, sc in each stitch to end of rnd.

Fasten off all colors. Weave in ends.

Large (make 2)

With Color A, ch29.

Rnd 1: Turn, sc in second chain from hook, sc8, sl st 3, sc6, hdc9, 6dc in last stitch, continue working on opposite side of chain, hdc9, sc6, sl st 3, sc9 sl st to first stitch to join rnd (60 sts).

Rnd 2: Ch1, 2sc in same stitch, sc11, hdc15, 2hdc in next 6 stitches, hdc15, sc11, 2sc in last stitch, sl st to first stitch to join rnd (68 sts).

Rnd 3: Ch1, sc in same stitch, 2sc in next stitch, sc11, hdc15, (hdc, 2hdc in next stitch) 6 times, hdc15, sc11, 2sc in next stitch, sc in last stitch, sl st to first stitch to join rnd (76 sts).

Rnd 4: Ch1, sc in same stitch, sc, 2sc in next stitch, sc17, hdc9, (hdc2, 2hdc in next stitch) 6 times, hdc9, sc17, 2sc in next stitch, sc2, sl st to first stitch to join rnd (84 sts).

Rnd 5: Ch1, sc in same stitch, sc2, 2sc in next stitch, sc12, hdc14, (sc3, 2sc in next stitch) 6 times, hdc14, sc12, 2sc in next stitch, sc3, sl st to first stitch to join rnd (92 sts).

Rnd 6: Drop Color A, join Color B, ch2, working in back loop only, fpdc31, (fpdc3, fpdc dec) 6 times, fpdc31, sl st to first stitch to join rnd (86 sts).

Rnd 7: Drop Color B, join Color C, ch2, fpdc31, (fpdc2, fpdc dec) 6 times, fpdc31, sl st to first stitch to join rnd (80 sts).

Rnd 8: Drop Color C, join Color D, ch2, fpdc31, (fpdc, fpdc dec) 6 times, fpdc31, sl st to first stitch to join rnd (74 sts).

Rnd 9: Drop Color D, pick up Color C, ch2, fpdc29, fpdc dec 8 times, fpdc29, sl st to first stitch to join rnd (66 sts).

Rnd 10: Drop Color C, pick up Color B, ch2, fpdc29, fpdc dec 4 times, fpdc29, sl st to first stitch to join rnd (62 sts).

Rnd 11: Drop Color B, pick up Color A, ch2, fpdc29, fpdc dec 2 times, fpdc29, sl st to first stitch to join rnd (60 sts).

Rnd 12: Ch1, sc20, ch7, sl st to stitch 32, turn, sl st each chain, sl st to stitch 21, sc in each stitch to end of rnd.

Fasten off all colors. Weave in ends.

Skill Level: Intermediate

Interlocking Rings Barefoot Sandals

Have fun in the sand with these beautiful sandals. They are perfect for a casual stroll on the beach or even a night at home!

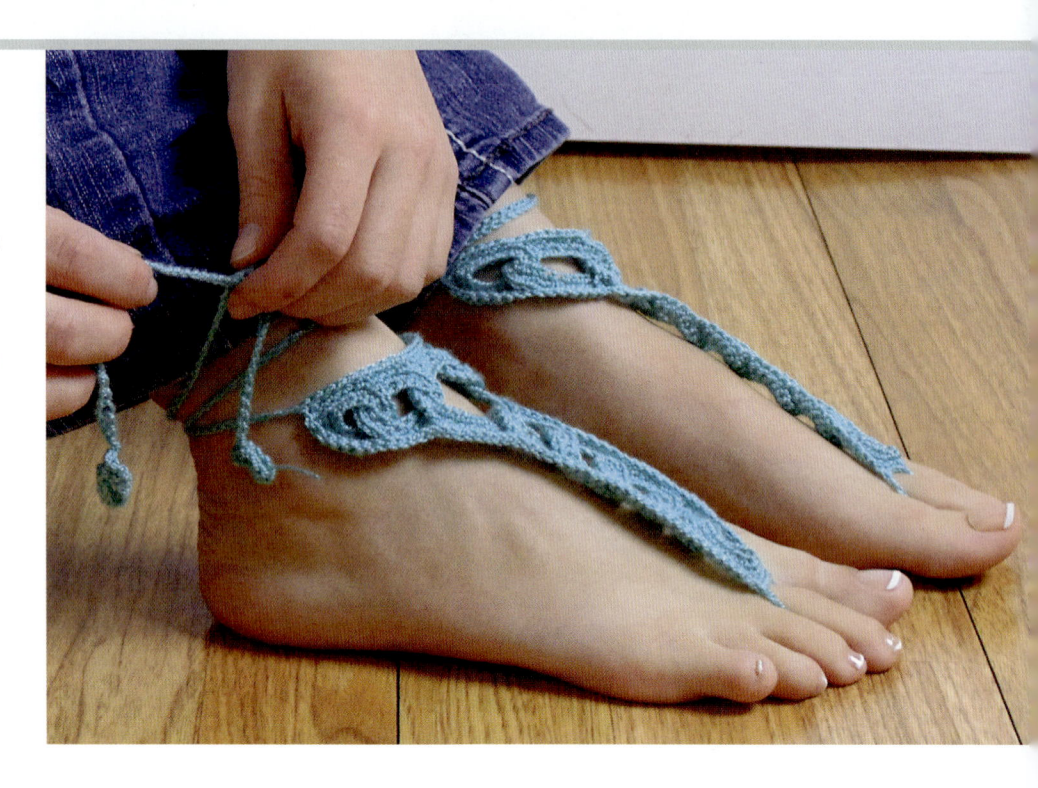

Finished Measurements
Women's Small: 4"/10 cm long, 4"/10 cm wide
Women's Medium/Large: 5"/12.75 cm long, 5"/12.75 cm wide

Yarn
- Bernat Handicrafter Crochet Thread #5, 100% acrylic (364 yd/333 m, 3 oz/85 g per skein)
  1 skein #16303131201 Stillwater

Hook and Other Materials
- US 8/1.5 mm steel crochet hook or size to obtain gauge
- 8 to 10 sewing pins
- Yarn needle

Gauge
24 sts and 24 rows in sc = 4"/10 cm square

Notes
- The sandal is made by linking the rings as they are crocheted, then finished with a single-crochet stitch trim.
- When joining the rings, insert the hook from front to back into the ring before slip stitching.

Small (make 2)

Ring 1
Ch16, sl st to ch1.
Rnd 1: Ch1, sc in each chain, sl st to first chain to join (16 sts).
Rnd 2: Ch1, *sc, 2sc in next stitch, repeat from * to complete rnd, sl st to first stitch to join (24 sts).
Fasten off. Weave in ends.

Rings 2–4
Ch16, insert hook in previous ring from front to back, sl st to first chain to join (16 sts).
NOTE: This joins each ring.
Rnd 1: Ch1, sc in each chain, sl st to first chain to join (16 sts).
Rnd 2: Ch1, *sc, 2sc in next stitch, repeat from * to complete rnd, sl st to first stitch to join (24 sts).
Fasten off. Weave in ends.

Ring 5
Ch24, insert hook in fourth ring from front to back, sl st to first chain to join (24 sts).
Rnd 1: Ch1, sc in each chain, sl st to first chain to join.
Rnd 2: Ch1, *sc, 2sc in next stitch, repeat from * to complete rnd, sl st to first stitch to join (36 sts).
Fasten off. Weave in ends.

Rings 6 & 7
NOTE: Both rings will be worked into Ring 5.
Ch21, insert hook in fifth ring from front to back, sl st to first chain to join (20 sts).
Rnd 1: Ch1, sc in each chain, sl st to first chain to join.
Rnd 2: Ch1, *sc, 2sc in next stitch, repeat from * to complete rnd, sl st to first stitch to join (30 sts).
Fasten off. Weave in ends.

Rings 8 & 9
NOTE: One ring will be worked into Ring 6 and the other will be worked into Ring 7.
Ch16, insert hook in ring from front to back, sl st to first chain to join (16 sts).
Rnd 1: Ch1, sc in each chain, sl st to first chain to join.
Rnd 2: Ch1, *sc, 2sc in next stitch, repeat from * to complete rnd, sl st to first stitch to join (24 sts).
Fasten off. Weave in ends.

Medium/Large (make 2)

Ring 1
Ch16, sl st to ch1.

Rnd 1: Ch1, sc in each chain, sl st to first chain to join (16 sts).

Rnd 2: Ch1, *sc, 2sc in next stitch, repeat from * to complete rnd, sl st to first stitch to join (24 sts).

Fasten off. Weave in ends.

Rings 2–5
Ch16, insert hook in previous ring from front to back, sl st to first chain to join (16 sts).

NOTE: This joins each ring.

Rnd 1: Ch1, sc in each chain, sl st to first chain to join.

Rnd 2: Ch1, *sc, 2sc in next stitch, repeat from * to complete rnd, sl st to first stitch to join (24 sts).

Fasten off. Weave in ends.

Ring 6
Ch24, insert hook in fourth ring from front to back, sl st to first chain to join (24 sts).

Rnd 1: Ch1, sc in each chain, sl st to first chain to join.

Rnd 2: Ch1, *sc, 2sc in next stitch, repeat from * to complete rnd, sl st to first stitch to join (36 sts).

Fasten off. Weave in ends.

Rings 7 & 8
NOTE: Both rings will be worked into Ring 6.

Ch20, insert hook in sixth ring from front to back, sl st to first chain to join (20 sts).

Rnd 1: Ch1, sc in each chain, sl st to first chain to join.

Rnd 2: Ch1, *sc, 2sc in next stitch, repeat from * to complete rnd, sl st to first stitch to join (30 sts).

Fasten off. Weave in ends.

Rings 9 & 10
NOTE: One ring will be worked into Ring 7 and the other will be worked into Ring 8.

Ch16, insert hook in ring from front to back, sl st to first chain to join (16 sts).

Rnd 1: Ch1, sc in each chain, sl st to first chain to join.

Rnd 2: Ch1, *sc, 2sc in next stitch, repeat from * to complete round, sl st to first stitch to join (24 sts).

Fasten off. Weave in ends.

Straps and Edging for Both Sizes

Pin the rings into place with the right sides all facing up.
NOTE: Position the joined slip stitch behind the previous ring when pinning so that the rings appear seamless.

Join yarn in ring on left. Ch1, sc in each stitch around the pinned sandal. There will be approximately 5 stitches on each side of Rings 1–4 when doing the edging. At the bottom of the stack of rings, ch14 (this creates the loop for your toe to go through), then continue to sc in each stitch around edge. When finished, sl st to first stitch to join.

Fasten off. Weave in ends.

For the two straps, working one at a time, join yarn at the top right and the top left of each sandal. For each strap, ch105, sl st to chain 100, ch1, 10sc in the ring, sl st to first stitch to join.

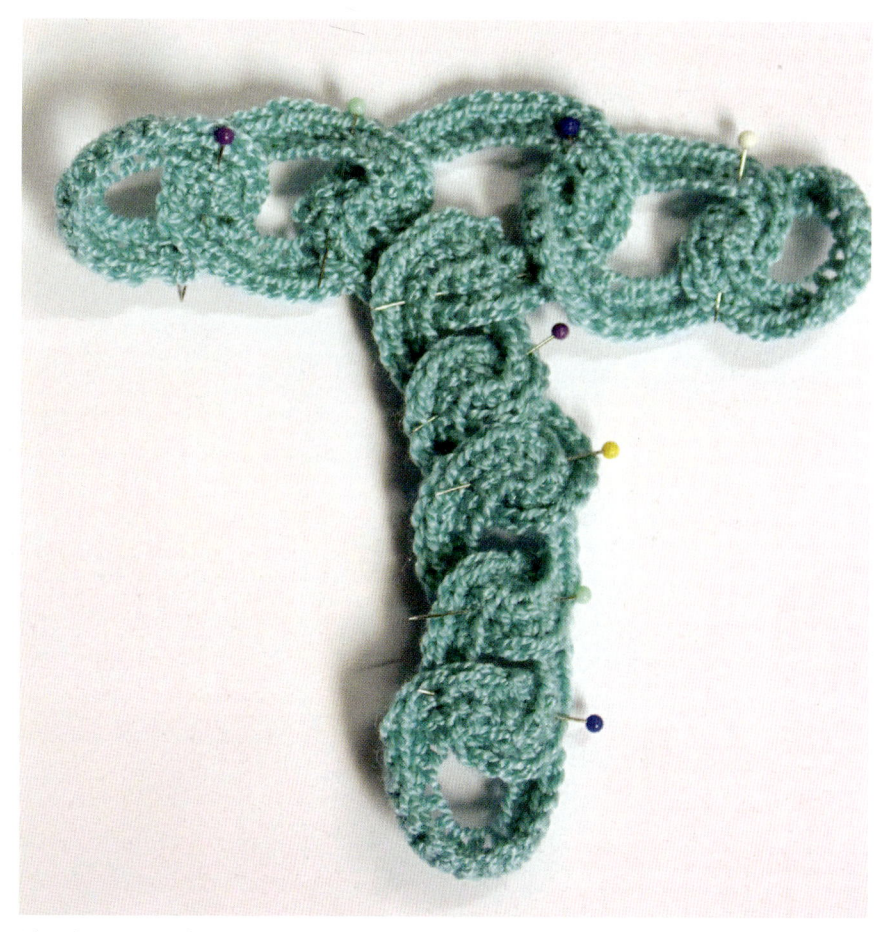

Fasten off. Weave in ends.

The rings pinned into place, ready to join the yarn for the straps and edging.

Skill Level: Intermediate

Ruby Red Slippers

Dress up or down. These fantastic slippers will be the cutest accessory in your little one's wardrobe!

Finished Measurements
Children's Small: 5"/12.75 cm long, 2"/5 cm wide
Children's Medium: 6"/15.25 cm long, 2"/5 cm wide
Children's Large: 7"/17.75 cm long, 2.5"/6 cm wide

Yarn
- Yarn Bee Fetching, bulky weight #5 yarn, 90% acrylic/10% metallic polyester (280 yd/256 m, 3.5 oz/100 g per skein)
  1 skein #2110 Ruby

Hook and Other Materials
- US E-4/3.5 mm crochet hook or size to obtain gauge
- Stitch marker
- Yarn needle

Gauge
20 sts and 20 rows in sc = 4"/10 cm square

Notes
- The slippers are worked in joined rounds from the center of the sole out.
- For tutorials on Front Post Double Crochet (fpdc), Front Post Double Crochet Decrease (fpdc dec), Front Post Double Crochet Decrease 3 Together (fpdc dec 3 tog), Single Crochet Decrease (sc dec), and Single Crochet Decrease 3 Together (sc dec 3 tog), see Stitch Guide (pages 83–101).

Small (make 2)
Ch15.
Rnd 1: Turn, sc in second chain from hook, sc4, hdc3, dc6, 7dc in last chain, continue working on opposite side of chain, dc6, hdc3, sc5, sl st to first stitch to join rnd (33 sts).
Rnd 2: Ch1, 2sc in same stitch, sc4, hdc3, dc6, 2dc in next 7 stitches, dc6, hdc3, sc4, sl st to first stitch to join rnd (42 sts).
Rnd 3: Ch1, sc in same stitch, 2sc in next stitch, hdc12, (hdc, 2hdc in next stitch) 7 times, hdc12, 2sc in last stitch, sl st to first stitch to join rnd (51 sts).
Rnd 4: Ch2, working in back loop only dc in each stitch, sl st to first stitch to join rnd.
Rnd 5: Ch2, fpdc15, (fpdc, fpdc dec) 7 times, fpdc15, sl st to first stitch to join rnd (44 sts).
Rnd 6: Ch2, fpdc15, fpdc dec 7 times, fpdc15, sl st to first stitch to join rnd (37 sts).
Rnd 7: Ch2, fpdc15, fpdc dec, fpdc dec 3 tog, fpdc dec, fpdc15, sl st to first stitch to join rnd (34 sts).
Rnd 8: Ch1, sc15, sc dec 3 tog, sc15, sl st to first stitch to join rnd (32 sts).
Rnd 9: Ch1, sl st 11, ch5, skip 9 stitches, sl st to next stitch, sl st 11, sl st to first stitch to join rnd (27 sts).
Fasten off. Weave in ends.

Medium (make 2)
Ch19.

Rnd 1: Turn, sc in second chain from hook, sc6, hdc3, dc7, 7dc in last chain, continue working on opposite side of chain, dc7, hdc3, sc6, sl st to first stitch to join rnd (41 sts).

Rnd 2: Ch1, 2sc in same stitch, sc6, hdc3, dc7, 2dc in next 7 stitches, dc7, hdc3, sc6, sl st to first stitch to join rnd (50 sts).

Rnd 3: Ch1, sc in same stitch, 2sc in next stitch, hdc16, (hdc, 2hdc in next stitch) 7 times, hdc16, 2sc in last stitch, sl st to first stitch to join rnd (59 sts).

Rnd 4: Ch2, working in back loop only dc in each stitch, sl st to first stitch to join rnd.

Rnd 5: Ch2, fpdc19, (fpdc, fpdc dec)7 times, fpdc19, sl st to first stitch to join rnd (52 sts).

Rnd 6: Ch2, fpdc19, fpdc dec 7 times, fpdc19, sl st to first stitch to join rnd (45 sts).

Rnd 7: Ch2, fpdc19, fpdc dec, fpdc dec 3 tog, fpdc dec, fpdc19, sl st to first stitch to join rnd (42 sts).

Rnd 8: Ch1, sc19, sc dec 3 tog, sc19, sl st to first stitch to join rnd (40 sts).

Rnd 9: Ch1, sl st 15, ch6, skip 9 stitches, sl st to next stitch, sl st 15, sl st to first stitch to join rnd (36 sts).

Fasten off. Weave in ends.

Large (make 2)
Ch23.

Rnd 1: Turn, sc in second chain from hook, sc8, hdc3, dc9, 7dc in last chain, continue working on opposite side of chain, dc9, hdc3, sc8, sl st to first stitch to join rnd (47 sts).

Rnd 2: Ch1, 2sc in same stitch, sc8, hdc3, dc9, 2dc in next 7 stitches, dc9, hdc3, sc8, sl st to first stitch to join rnd (56 sts).

Rnd 3: Ch1, sc in same stitch, 2sc in next stitch, hdc20, (hdc, 2hdc in next stitch) 7 times, hdc20, 2sc in last stitch, sl st to first stitch to join rnd (65 sts).

Rnd 4: Ch2, working in back loop only dc in each stitch, sl st to first stitch to join rnd.

Rnd 5: Ch2, fpdc23, (fpdc, fpdc dec) 7 times, fpdc23, sl st to first stitch to join rnd (58 sts).

Rnd 6: Ch2, fpdc23, fpdc dec 7 times, fpdc23, sl st to first stitch to join rnd (51 sts).

Rnd 7: Ch2, fpdc23, fpdc dec, fpdc dec 3 tog, fpdc dec, fpdc23, sl st to first stitch to join rnd (48 sts).

Rnd 8: Ch1, sc23, sc dec 3 tog, sc23, sl st to first stitch to join rnd (46 sts).

Rnd 9: Ch1, sl st 19, ch6, skip 9 stitches, sl st to next stitch, sl st 19, sl st to first stitch to join rnd (44 sts).

Fasten off. Weave in ends.

Bow for All Sizes (make 2)
Ch25.

Row 1: Turn, sc in second chain from hook and in each across (24 sts).

Rows 2–3: Turn, ch1, sc in each stitch.

Fasten off, leaving a 10"/25 cm tail.

Using yarn needle, sew ends together.

Wrap yarn still on the yarn needle around center of bow 10 to 15 times and secure it so that the wrapped yarn won't unravel. Fasten off.

Using yarn needle, sew onto front of each slipper.

Skill Level: Intermediate

Fabulous Faux Cable Loafers

57

Made with doubled-up strands of crochet thread, these loafers are super soft and cozy. They are fun to crochet and even more fun to wear!

Finished Measurements
Women's Small: 8"/20.5 cm long, 3.5"/8.9 cm wide
Women's Medium: 9"/23 cm long, 4"/10cm wide
Women's Large: 10"/25.5 cm long, 4"/10cm wide

Yarn
- Bernat Handicrafter Crochet Thread Size 5, 100% acrylic (371 yd/339 m, 3 oz/85 g per skein)
  2 skeins #31134 Really Royal

Hook and Other Materials
- US E-4/3.5 mm crochet hook or size to obtain gauge
- Stitch marker
- Yarn needle
- 2 medium cream buttons
- Sewing thread in matching color and needle

Gauge
Holding 2 strands together, 10 sts and 12 rows in sc = 2"/5 cm square

Notes
- The shoes are crocheted holding 2 strands of yarn together.
- The side and top panels and sole are crocheted separately and then sewn together to complete the loafer. The right side of the panel is the side with the faux cable.
- The sole is worked from the center out in joined rounds. If you like, mark the beginning of the round with a stitch marker.
- When joining the rounds for the sole, the slip stitch will not count as a stitch.
- For a tutorial on Single Crochet Decrease (sc dec), see page 87.

Small (make 2)

Side Panel
Holding 2 strands of yarn together, ch10.
Row 1: Turn, sc in second chain from hook and in each chain across (9 sts).
Row 2: Turn, ch1, sc4, ch12, sc in the next stitch, sc3 (20 sts).
Row 3: Turn, ch1, sc4, sl st 12 in the ch12 space, sc4.
Row 4: Turn, ch1, sc4, skip the 12 stitch loop, sc4 (8 sts).
Rows 5–83: Repeat Rows 2–4.
Row 84: Turn, ch1, sc in each stitch.
Fasten off. Weave in ends.

Top Panel
Holding 2 strands of yarn together, ch14.
Row 1: Turn, sc in second chain from hook and in each chain across (13 sts).
Row 2: Turn, ch1, sc13.
Row 3: Turn, ch1, in front loop only, sc13.
Rows 4–6: Turn, ch1, sc in each stitch.
Row 7: Turn, ch1, sc, sc dec, sc7, sc dec, sc (11 sts).
Row 8: Turn, ch1, sc in each stitch.
Row 9: Turn, ch1, sc, sc dec, sc5, sc dec, sc (9 sts).
Row 10: Turn, ch1, sc in each stitch.
Row 11: Turn, ch1, sc, sc dec, sc3, sc dec, sc (7 sts).
Row 12: Turn, ch1, sc in each stitch.
Row 13: Turn, ch1, sc, sc dec, sc1, sc dec, sc (5 sts).
Row 14: Turn, ch1, sc in each stitch.
Fasten off. Weave in ends.

Sole
Holding 2 strands of yarn together, ch26.
Rnd 1: Turn, sc in second chain from hook, sc9, dc14, 6dc in last chain, continue working on opposite side of chain dc14, sc10, sl st to first stitch to join rnd (54 sts).
Rnd 2: Ch1, 2sc in same stitch as ch1, hdc17, dc8, 2dc in next 6 stitches, dc8, hdc17, 2sc in last stitch, sl st to first stitch to join rnd (62 sts).
Rnd 3: Ch1, sc in same stitch as ch1, 2sc in next stitch, hdc17, dc8, *dc, 2dc in next stitch, repeat from * 5 more times, dc8, hdc17, 2sc in next stitch, sc in last stitch, sl st to first stitch of rnd to join (70 sts).

Rnd 4: Ch1, sc in same stitch as ch1, sc, 2sc in next stitch, hdc8, dc17, * dc2, 2dc in next stitch, repeat from * 5 more times, dc17, hdc8, 2sc in next stitch, sc2, sl st to first stitch of rnd to join (78 sts).

Rnd 5: Ch1, sc in same stitch as ch1, sc2, 2sc in next stitch, hdc32, 2hdc in next stitch, hdc8, 2hdc in next stitch, hdc32, 2sc in next stitch, sc3, sl st to first stitch of rnd to join (82 sts).

Fasten off. Weave in ends.

Medium (make 2)
Side Panel
Holding 2 strands of yarn together, ch10.

Row 1: Turn, sc in second chain from hook and in each chain across (9 sts).

Row 2: Turn, ch1, sc4, ch12, sc in the next stitch, sc3 (20 sts).

Row 3: Turn, ch1, sc4, sl st 12 in the ch12 space, sc4.

Row 4: Turn, ch1, sc4, skip the 12 stitch loop, sc4 (8 sts).

Rows 5–89: Repeat Rows 2–4.

Row 90: Turn, ch1, sc in each stitch.

Fasten off. Weave in ends.

Top Panel
Holding 2 strands of yarn together, ch16.

Row 1: Turn, sc in second chain from hook and in each chain across (15 sts).

Row 2: Turn, ch1, sc15.

Row 3: Turn, ch1, in front loop only, sc15.

Rows 4–6: Turn, ch1, sc in each stitch.

Row 7: Turn, ch1, sc, sc dec, sc9, sc dec, sc (13 sts).

Row 8: Turn, ch1, sc in each stitch.

Row 9: Turn, ch1, sc, sc dec, sc7, sc dec, sc (11 sts).

Row 10: Turn, ch1, sc in each stitch.

Row 11: Turn, ch1, sc, sc dec, sc5, sc dec, sc (9 sts).

Row 12: Turn, ch1, sc in each stitch.

Row 13: Turn, ch1, sc, sc dec, sc3, sc dec, sc (7 sts).

Row 14: Turn, ch1, sc in each stitch.

Fasten off. Weave in ends.

Sole
Holding 2 strands of yarn together, ch30.

Rnd 1: Turn, sc in second chain from hook, sc11, dc16, 6dc in last chain, continue working on opposite side of chain dc16, sc12, sl st to first stitch to join rnd (62 sts).

Rnd 2: Ch1, 2sc in same stitch as ch1, hdc18, dc9, 2dc in next 6 stitches, dc9, hdc18, 2sc in last stitch, sl st to first stitch to join rnd (70 sts).

Rnd 3: Ch1, sc in same stitch as ch1, 2sc in next stitch, hdc18, dc9, *dc, 2dc in next stitch, repeat from * 5 more times, dc9, hdc18, 2sc in next stitch, sc in last stitch, sl st to first stitch of rnd to join (78 sts).

Rnd 4: Ch1, sc in same stitch as ch1, sc, 2sc in next stitch, hdc9, dc18, *dc2, 2dc in next stitch, repeat from * 5 more times, dc18, hdc9, 2sc in next stitch, sc2, sl st to first stitch of rnd to join (86 sts).

Rnd 5: Ch1, sc in same stitch as ch1, sc2, 2sc in next stitch, hdc34, 2hdc in next stitch, hdc11, 2hdc in next stitch, hdc34, 2sc in next stitch, sc3, sl st to first stitch of rnd to join (90 sts).

Fasten off. Weave in ends.

Large (make 2)
Side Panel
Holding 2 strands of yarn together, ch10.

Row 1: Turn, sc in second chain from hook and in each chain across (9 sts).

Row 2: Turn, ch1, sc4, ch12, sc in the next stitch, sc3 (20 sts).

Row 3: Turn, ch1, sc4, sl st 12 in the ch12 space, sc4.

Row 4: Turn, ch1, sc4, skip the 12 stitch loop, sc4 (8 sts).

Rows 5–103: Repeat Rows 2–4.

Row 104: Turn, ch1, sc in each stitch.

Fasten off. Weave in ends.

Top Panel
Holding 2 strands of yarn together, ch16.

Row 1: Turn, sc in second chain from hook and in each chain across (15 sts).

Row 2: Turn, ch1, sc15.

Row 3: Turn, ch1, in front loop only, sc15.

Rows 4–6: Turn, ch1, sc in each stitch.

Row 7: Turn, ch1, sc, sc dec, sc9, sc dec, sc (13 sts).

Row 8: Turn, ch1, sc in each stitch.

Row 9: Turn, ch1, sc, sc dec, sc7, sc dec, sc (11 sts).

Row 10: Turn, ch1, sc in each stitch.

Row 11: Turn, ch1, sc, sc dec, sc5, sc dec, sc (9 sts).

Row 12: Turn, ch1, sc in each stitch.

Row 13: Turn, ch1, sc, sc dec, sc3, sc dec, sc (7 sts).

Row 14: Turn, ch1, sc in each stitch.

Fasten off. Weave in ends.

Sole

Holding 2 strands of yarn together, ch34.

Rnd 1: Turn, sc in second chain from hook, sc13, dc18, 6dc in last chain, continue working on opposite side of chain dc18, sc14, sl st to first stitch to join rnd (70 sts).

Rnd 2: Ch1, 2sc in same stitch as ch1, hdc20, dc11, 2dc in next 6 stitches, dc11, hdc20, 2sc in last stitch, sl st to first stitch to join rnd (78 sts).

Rnd 3: Ch1, sc in same stitch as ch1, 2sc in next stitch, hdc18, dc11, *dc, 2dc in next stitch, repeat from * 5 more times, dc11, hdc18, 2sc in next stitch, sc in last stitch, sl st to first stitch of rnd to join (86 sts).

Rnd 4: Ch1, sc in same stitch as ch1, sc, 2sc in next stitch, hdc11, dc20, *dc2, 2dc in next stitch, repeat from * 5 more times, dc20, hdc11, 2sc in next stitch, sc2, sl st to first stitch of rnd to join (94 sts).

Rnd 5: Ch1, sc in same stitch as ch1, sc2, 2sc in next stitch, hdc38, 2hdc in next stitch, hdc8, 2hdc in next stitch, hdc38, 2sc in next stitch, sc3, sl st to first stitch of rnd to join (98 sts).

Fasten off. Weave in ends.

Assembly for All Sizes

With sole laying face up, join the side panel, right side facing out, on the left side three quarters of the way up the sole. Whip stitch the two pieces together to join. Next, assemble the loops by taking the second loop made and pulling it from the back to front and continue by pulling the next loop through the back of the current loop. Secure the last loop with the yarn needle to complete. Sew a button onto the center loop on the side of the top panel on the opposite sides of each loafer to designate the right and left loafer.

Next, in front center of the shoe, line up the bottom of the top section with the back exposed loop from Row 3 facing downward. Secure with stitch markers. Whip stitch it onto the side panel.

Fasten off. Weave in ends.

Last, take the yarn needle and stitch over the top whip-stitch seam to add a finishing detail.

Fasten off. Weave in ends.

Skill Level: Intermediate

Owl Boots

61

These boots are such a hoot! His feathers are made using the crocodile stitch. Have fun making them in a variety of sizes and colors!

Finished Measurements
Children's Small: 5"/12.75 cm long, 2"/5cm wide
Children's Medium: 6"/15.25 cm long, 2"/5cm wide
Children's Large: 7"/17.75 cm long, 2.5"/6cm wide

Yarn
- Lion Brand Vanna's Choice, medium worsted weight #4 yarn, 100% acrylic (170 yd/156 m, 3.5 oz/100 g per skein)
   1 skein #860-123 Beige (Color A)
   1 skein #860-147 Purple (Color B)
   1 skein #860-171 Fern (Color C)
   1 skein #860-100 White (Color D)
   1 skein #860-135 Rust (Color E)

Hook and Other Materials
- US E-4/3.5 mm crochet hook or size to obtain gauge
- Stitch marker
- Yarn needle
- 4 small brown buttons
- Sewing thread in matching color and needle

Gauge
8 sts and 6 rows in hdc = 2"/5 cm square

Notes
- The slippers are worked from the center of the sole out in joined rounds.
- For tutorials on Half Double Crochet Decrease (hdc dec) and Double Crochet Decrease (dc dec), see pages 88 and 90.

Small (make 2)
Using Color A, ch14.

Rnd 1: Turn, sc in second chain from hook, sc3, hdc4, dc4, 6dc in last chain, continue working on opposite side of chain dc4, hdc4, sc4, sl st to first stitch to join rnd (30 sts).

Rnd 2: Ch1, 2sc in same stitch, sc3, hdc8, 2hdc in next 6 stitches, hdc8, sc3, 2sc in last stitch, sl st to first stitch to join rnd (38 sts).

Rnd 3: Ch1, sc in same stitch, 2sc in next stitch, sc2, hdc9, *hdc, 2hdc in next stitch, repeat from * 5 more times, hdc9, sc2, 2sc in last stitch, sl st to first stitch to join rnd (44 sts).

Rnd 4: Ch1, sc2, 2sc, sc11, *hdc2, 2hdc in next stitch, repeat from * 5 more times, sc11, 2sc in next stitch, sc2, sl st to first stitch to join rnd (52 sts).

Rnd 5: Ch2, working in back loop only (blo), hdc in each stitch, sl st to first stitch to join rnd (52 sts).

Rnd 6: Ch2, hdc17, *hdc2, hdc dec, repeat from * 7 more times, hdc17, sl st to first stitch to join rnd (44 sts).

Rnd 7: Ch2, hdc17, *hdc, hdc dec, repeat from * 7 more times, hdc17, sl st to first stitch to join (38 sts).

Rnd 8: Ch2, hdc17, *dc dec, repeat from * 7 more times, hdc17, sl st to first stitch to join (30 sts).

Rnd 9: Ch2, hdc15, *dc dec, repeat from * 5 more times, hdc15, sl st to first stitch to join rnd (24 sts).

Rnd 10: Ch2, hdc dec, hdc13, *dc dec, repeat from * 2 more times, hdc15, sl st to first stitch to join rnd (20 sts).

Rnd 11: Fasten off Color A, join Color B, ch3, dc in same stitch, skip 1 stitch, *2dc in next stitch, skip 1 stitch, repeat from * to complete rnd, sl st to center of first ch3 and dc set to join rnd.

Rnd 12: Ch3 (counts as the first dc), using the first dc post, 3dc down the post, ch1, 4dc up the next dc post, skip 1 set of 2dc, *on next 2dc set, 4dc down the first dc post, ch1, 4dc up the next post, skip the next set of 2dc, repeat from * to complete rnd, sl st to third chain of first dc in center of last skipped 2dc to join (90 sts).

Rnd 13: Fasten off Color B, join Color C, ch3, dc in same stitch, *2dc in center of worked 2dc set, 2dc over the work in the next unworked 2dc set, repeat from * to complete rnd, sl st to center of first ch3 and dc set to join (20 sts).

Rnd 14: Ch3 (counts as first dc), using the first dc post, 3dc down the post, ch1, 4dc up the next dc post, skip 1 set of 2dc, *on next 2dc set, 4dc down the first dc post, ch1, 4dc up the next post, skip the next set of 2dc, repeat from * to complete round, sl st to third chain of first dc in center of last skipped 2dc to join (90 sts).

Rnd 15: Fasten off Color C, join Color A, ch3, dc in same stitch, *2dc in center of worked 2dc set, 2dc over the work in the next unworked 2dc set, repeat from * to complete rnd, sl st to center of first ch3 and dc set to join (20 sts).

Rnd 16: Ch3 (counts as first dc), using the first dc post, 3dc down the post, ch1, 4dc up the next dc post, skip 1 set of 2dc, *on next 2dc set, 4dc down the first dc post, ch1, 4dc up the next post, skip the next set of 2dc, repeat from * to complete rnd, sl st to third chain of first dc in center of last skipped 2dc to join (90 sts).

Rnd 17: Ch3, dc in same stitch, *2dc in center of worked 2dc set, 2dc over the work in the next unworked 2dc set, repeat from * to complete rnd, sl st to center of first ch3 and dc set to join (20 sts).

Rnds 18–22: Ch2, hdc in each stitch, sl st to first stitch to join.

Fasten off. Weave in ends.

Medium (make 2)

Using Color A, ch18.

Rnd 1: Turn, sc in second chain from hook, sc4, hdc5, dc6, 6dc in last chain, continue working on opposite side of chain dc6, hdc5, sc5, sl st to first stitch to join rnd (38 sts).

Rnd 2: Ch1, 2sc in same stitch, sc4, hdc11, 2hdc in next 6 stitches, hdc11, sc4, 2sc in last stitch, sl st to first stitch to join rnd (46 sts).

Rnd 3: Ch1, sc in same stitch, 2sc in next stitch, sc3, hdc12, *hdc, 2hdc in next stitch, repeat from * 5 more times, hdc12, sc3, 2sc in last stitch, sl st to first stitch to join rnd (54 sts).

Rnd 4: Ch1, sc2, 2sc, sc15, *hdc2, 2hdc in next stitch, repeat from * 5 more times, sc15, 2sc in next stitch, sc2, sl st to first stitch to join rnd (62 sts).

Rnd 5: Ch2, working in the back loop only (blo), hdc in each stitch, sl st to first stitch to join rnd (62 sts).

Rnd 6: Ch2, hdc17, *hdc2, hdc dec, repeat from * 7 more times, hdc17, sl st to first stitch to join rnd (54 sts).

Rnd 7: Ch2, hdc17, *hdc, hdc dec, repeat from * 7 more times, hdc17, sl st to first stitch to join rnd (46 sts).

Rnd 8: Ch2, hdc17, *dc dec, repeat from * 7 more times, hdc17, sl st to first stitch to join rnd (34 sts).

Rnd 9: Ch2, hdc15, *dc dec, repeat from * 5 more times, hdc15, sl st to first stitch to join rnd (28 sts).

Rnd 10: Ch2, hdc dec, hdc15, *dc dec, repeat from * 2 more times, hdc15, sl st to first stitch to join rnd (24 sts).

Rnd 11: Fasten off Color A, join Color B, ch3, dc in same stitch, skip 1 stitch, *2dc in next stitch, skip 1 stitch, repeat from * to complete rnd, sl st to center of first ch3 and dc set to join.

Rnd 12: Ch3 (counts as first dc), using the first dc post, 3dc down the post, ch1, 4dc up the next dc post, skip 1 set of 2dc, *on next 2dc set, 4dc down the first dc post, ch1, 4dc up the next post, skip the next set of 2dc, repeat from * to complete rnd, sl st to third chain of first dc in center of last skipped 2dc to join (108 sts).

Rnd 13: Fasten off Color B, join Color C, ch3, dc in same stitch, *2dc in center of worked 2dc set, 2dc over the work in the next unworked 2dc set, repeat from * to complete rnd, sl st to center of first ch3 and dc set to join (24 sts).

Rnd 14: Ch3 (counts as first dc), using the first dc post, 3dc down the post, ch1, 4dc up the next dc post, skip 1 set of 2dc, *on next 2dc set, 4dc down the first dc post, ch1, 4dc up the next post, skip the next set of 2dc, repeat from * to complete rnd, sl st to third chain of first dc in center of last skipped 2dc to join (108 sts).

Rnd 15: Fasten off Color C, join Color A, ch3, dc in same stitch, *2dc in center of worked 2dc set, 2dc over the work in the next unworked 2dc set, repeat from * to complete rnd, sl st to center of first ch3 and dc set to join (24 sts).

Rnd 16: Ch3 (counts as first dc), using the first dc post, 3dc down the post, ch1, 4dc up the next dc post, skip 1 set of 2dc, *on next 2dc set, 4dc down the first dc post, ch1, 4dc up the next post, skip the next set of 2dc, repeat from * to complete rnd, sl st to third chain of first dc in center of last skipped 2dc to join (108 sts).

Rnd 17: Ch3, dc in same stitch, *2dc in center of worked 2dc set, 2dc over the work in the next unworked 2dc set, repeat from * to complete rnd, sl st to center of first ch3 and dc set to join (24 sts).

Rnds 18–22: Ch2, hdc in each stitch, sl st to first stitch to join rnd.

Fasten off. Weave in ends.

Large (make 2)

Using Color A, ch22.

Rnd 1: Turn, sc in second chain from hook, sc6, hdc6, dc7, 6dc in last chain, continue working on opposite side of chain dc7, hdc6, sc7, sl st to first stitch to join rnd (46 sts).

Rnd 2: Ch1, 2sc in same stitch, sc6, hdc13, 2hdc in next 6 stitches, hdc13, sc6, 2sc in last stitch, sl st to first stitch to join rnd (54 sts).

Rnd 3: Ch1, sc in same stitch, 2sc in next stitch, sc5, hdc14, *hdc, 2hdc in next stitch, repeat from * 5 more times, hdc14, sc5, 2sc in last stitch, sl st to first stitch to join rnd (62 sts).

Rnd 4: Ch1, sc2, 2sc, sc19, *hdc2, 2hdc in next stitch, repeat from * 5 more times, sc19, 2sc in next stitch, sc2, sl st to first stitch to join rnd (70 sts).

Rnd 5: Ch2, working in the back loop only, hdc in each stitch, sl st to first stitch to join rnd (70 sts).

Rnd 6: Ch2, hdc21, *hdc2, hdc dec, repeat from * 7 more times, hdc17, sl st to first stitch to join rnd (62 sts).

Rnd 7: Ch2, hdc21, *hdc, hdc dec, repeat from * 7 more times, hdc17, sl st to first stitch to join rnd (54 sts).

Rnd 8: Ch2, hdc21, *dc dec, repeat from * 7 more times, hdc17, sl st to first stitch to join rnd (46 sts).

Rnd 9: Ch2, hdc19, *dc dec, repeat from * 5 more times, hdc19, sl st to first stitch to join rnd (40 sts).

Rnd 10: Ch2, hdc dec, hdc19, *dc dec, repeat from * 2 more times, hdc19, sl st to first stitch to join rnd (36 sts).

Rnd 11: Fasten off Color A, join Color B, ch3, dc in same stitch, skip 1 stitch, *2dc in next stitch, skip 1 stitch, repeat from * to complete rnd, sl st to center of first ch3 and dc set to join (36 sts).

Rnd 12: Ch3 (counts as first dc), using the first dc post, 3dc down the post, ch1, 4dc up the next dc post, skip 1 set of 2dc, *on next 2dc set, 4dc down the first dc post, ch1, 4dc up the next post, skip the next set of 2dc, repeat from * to complete rnd, sl st to third chain of first dc in center of last skipped 2dc to join (162 sts).

Rnd 13: Fasten off Color B, join Color C, ch3, dc in same stitch, *2dc in center of worked 2dc set, 2dc over work in the next unworked 2dc set, repeat from * to complete rnd, sl st to center of first ch3 and dc set to join (36 sts).

Rnd 14: Ch3 (counts as first dc), using the first dc post, 3dc down the post, ch1, 4dc up the next dc post, skip 1 set of 2dc, *on next 2dc set, 4dc down the first dc post, ch1, 4dc up the next post, skip the next set of 2dc, repeat from * to complete rnd, sl st to third chain of first dc in center of last skipped 2dc to join (162 sts).

Rnd 15: Fasten off Color C, join Color A, ch3, dc in same stitch, *2dc in center of worked 2dc set, 2dc over work in next unworked 2dc set, repeat from * to complete rnd, sl st to center of first ch3 and dc set to join (36 sts).

Rnd 16: Ch3 (counts as first dc), using the first dc post, 3dc down the post, ch1, 4dc up the next dc post, skip 1 set of 2dc, *on next 2dc set, 4dc down the first dc post, ch1, 4dc up the next post, skip the next set of 2dc, repeat from * to complete rnd, sl st to third chain of first dc in center of last skipped 2dc to join (162 sts).

Rnd 17: Ch3 (counts as first dc), dc in same stitch, *2dc in center of worked 2dc set, 2dc over work in the next unworked 2dc set, repeat from * to complete rnd, sl st to center of first ch3 and dc set to join (36 sts).

Rnds 18–22: Ch2, hdc in each stitch, sl st to first stitch to join rnd.

Fasten off. Weave in ends.

Eyes for All Sizes

Back (make 2)

Using Color B, ch2.

Rnd 1: 6sc in first chain (6 sts).

Rnd 2: Working continuously in the round, 2sc in each stitch (12 sts).

Rnd 3: *Sc, 2sc in the next stitch, repeat from * to complete rnd (18 sts).

Fasten off, leaving a 10"/25.5 cm tail.

Top (make 2)

Using Color D, ch2

Rnd 1: 6sc in first chain (6 sts).

Rnd 2: Working continuously in the round, 2sc in each stitch (12 sts).

Fasten off, leaving a 10"/25.5 cm tail.

Finishing for All Sizes

Using yarn needle, sew the back part of the eye onto the side of the boot. Next, sew the top of the eye onto the back. Repeat for the other boot.

Using sewing needle and thread, sew a small button onto each of the eyes.

Using yarn needle and Color E, stitch a triangle nose in between the eyes.

Last, cut 4 (3"/7.75 cm) lengths each of Colors B and C. Take 2 of each color and apply to the outside of each eye like you would fringe (pull the center of the yarn through the stitch, then pull the ends through the center loop and pull tight). Trim evenly.

Skill Level: Beginner

Elfin Boot Slippers

These are a must for the holidays! And you can crochet them in different colors to play fairies or elves!

Finished Measurements

Children's Small: 8"/20.5 cm long (5"/12.75 cm foot space), 3"/7.75 cm wide

Children's Medium: 9"/23 cm long (6"/15.25 cm foot space), 3.5"/9 cm wide

Children's Large: 10"/25 cm long (7"/17.75 cm foot space), 4"/10 cm wide

Yarn

- Red Heart Soft, medium worsted weight #4 yarn, 100% acrylic (256 yd/234 m, 5 oz/141 g per skein)
  1 skein #9779 Berry (Color A)
  1 skein #4601 Off White (Color B)

Hook and Other Materials

- US F-5/3.75 mm crochet hook or size to obtain gauge
- Stitch marker
- Yarn needle

Gauge

16 sts and 14 rows in hdc = 4"/10 cm square

Notes

- Each slipper is worked from the toe to the heel continuously in the round, then in rows to finish. The cuff is added after the base shoe is complete.
- Use a stitch marker to mark the beginning of the round.

Small (make 2)

Body of Slipper

Using Color A, ch3, sl st to first chain to join.

Rnd 1: Ch2, 4hdc in ring (4 sts).
Rnd 2: Working continuously in the round, hdc4.
Rnd 3: 2hdc in next stitch, hdc3 (5 sts).
Rnd 4: Hdc5.
Rnd 5: 2hdc in next stitch, hdc4 (6 sts).
Rnd 6: Hdc6.
Rnd 7: 2hdc in next stitch, hdc5 (7 sts).
Rnd 8: Hdc7.
Rnd 9: 2hdc in next stitch, hdc6 (8 sts).
Rnd 10: 2hdc in next stitch, hdc7 (9 sts).
Rnd 11: 2hdc in next stitch, hdc8 (10 sts).
Rnd 12: 2hdc in next stitch, hdc9 (11 sts).
Rnd 13: 2hdc in next stitch, hdc10 (12 sts).
Rnd 14: 2hdc in next stitch, hdc11 (13 sts).
Rnd 15: 2hdc in next stitch, hdc12 (14 sts).
Rnd 16: 2hdc in next stitch, hdc13 (15 sts).
Rnd 17: 2hdc in next stitch, hdc14 (16 sts).
Rnd 18: 2hdc in next stitch, hdc15 (17 sts).
Rnd 19: 2hdc in next stitch, hdc16 (18 sts).
Rnd 20: 2hdc in next stitch, hdc17 (19 sts).
Rnd 21: 2hdc in next stitch, hdc18 (20 sts).
Rnd 22: 2hdc in next stitch, hdc19 (21 sts).
Rnd 23: 2hdc in next stitch, hdc20 (22 sts).
Rnd 24: Hdc22.
Rnd 25: Hdc22, sl st to first stitch of rnd to join.
Rows 26–32: Turn, ch2, hdc18 (18 sts).
Fasten off, leaving a long tail.
Turn work wrong side out. With yarn needle, sew heel together.

Cuff

Turn work right side out.

Rnd 1: Using Color A, join yarn at seam for the heel, using ends of rows as stitches, ch2, hdc24, sl st to first stitch to join (20 sts).
Rnds 2–3: Working continuously in the round, ch2, hdc20.
Row 4: Turn, ch2, in back loop only, hdc20, do not join.
Rows 5–6: Turn, ch2, hdc20.
Row 7: Fasten off Color A, join Color B, ch1, sl st in each stitch.
Row 8: Ch3, sl st to same stitch, *sl st to next stitch, ch3, sl st to same stitch, repeat from * to complete row.
Fasten off. Weave in ends.

Medium (make 2)
Body of Slipper

Using Color A, ch3, sl st to first chain to join.
Rnd 1: Ch2, 4hdc in ring (4 sts).
Rnd 2: Working continuously in the round, hdc4.
Rnd 3: 2hdc in next stitch, hdc3 (5 sts).
Rnd 4: Hdc5.
Rnd 5: 2hdc in next stitch, hdc4 (6 sts).
Rnd 6: Hdc6.
Rnd 7: 2hdc in next stitch, hdc5 (7 sts).
Rnd 8: Hdc7.
Rnd 9: 2hdc in next stitch, hdc6 (8 sts).
Rnd 10: 2hdc in next stitch, hdc7 (9 sts).
Rnd 11: 2hdc in next stitch, hdc8 (10 sts).
Rnd 12: 2hdc in next stitch, hdc9 (11 sts).
Rnd 13: 2hdc in next stitch, hdc10 (12 sts).
Rnd 14: 2hdc in next stitch, hdc11 (13 sts).
Rnd 15: 2hdc in next stitch, hdc12 (14 sts).
Rnd 16: 2hdc in next stitch, hdc13 (15 sts).
Rnd 17: 2hdc in next stitch, hdc14 (16 sts).
Rnd 18: 2hdc in next stitch, hdc15 (17 sts).
Rnd 19: 2hdc in next stitch, hdc16 (18 sts).
Rnd 20: 2hdc in next stitch, hdc17 (19 sts).
Rnd 21: 2hdc in next stitch, hdc18 (20 sts).
Rnd 22: 2hdc in next stitch, hdc19 (21 sts).
Rnd 23: 2hdc in next stitch, hdc20 (22 sts).
Rnd 24: 2hdc in next stitch, hdc21 (23 sts).
Rnd 25: 2hdc in next stitch, hdc22 (24 sts).
Rnd 26–29: Hdc24.
Rnd 30: Hdc24, sl st to first stitch of rnd to join.
Rows 31–39: Turn, ch2, hdc18 (18 sts).
Fasten off.
Turn work wrong side out. With yarn needle, sew heel together.

Cuff
Turn work right side out.
Rnd 1: Using Color A, join yarn at seam, using ends of rows as stitches, ch2, hdc24, sl st to first stitch to join (24 sts).
Rnds 2–3: Working continuously in the round, ch2, hdc24.
Row 4: Turn, ch2, using back loop only, hdc24, do not join.
Rows 5–8: Turn, ch2, hdc24.
Row 9: Fasten off Color A, join Color B, ch1, sl st in each stitch.
Row 10: Ch3, sl st to same stitch, *sl st to next stitch, ch3, sl st to same stitch, repeat from * to complete row.
Fasten off. Weave in ends.

Large (make 2)
Body of Slipper

Using Color A, ch3, sl st to first chain to join.
Rnd 1: Ch2, 4hdc in ring (4 sts).
Rnd 2: Working continuously in the round, hdc4.
Rnd 3: 2hdc in next stitch, hdc3 (5 sts).
Rnd 4: Hdc5.
Rnd 5: 2hdc in next stitch, hdc4 (6 sts).
Rnd 6: Hdc6.
Rnd 7: 2hdc in next stitch, hdc5 (7 sts).
Rnd 8: Hdc7.
Rnd 9: 2hdc in next stitch, hdc6 (8 sts).
Rnd 10: 2hdc in next stitch, hdc7 (9 sts).
Rnd 11: 2hdc in next stitch, hdc8 (10 sts).
Rnd 12: 2hdc in next stitch, hdc9 (11 sts).
Rnd 13: 2hdc in next stitch, hdc10 (12 sts).
Rnd 14: 2hdc in next stitch, hdc11 (13 sts).
Rnd 15: 2hdc in next stitch, hdc12 (14 sts).
Rnd 16: 2hdc in next stitch, hdc13 (15 sts).
Rnd 17: 2hdc in next stitch, hdc14 (16 sts).
Rnd 18: 2hdc in next stitch, hdc15 (17 sts).
Rnd 19: 2hdc in next stitch, hdc16 (18 sts).
Rnd 20: 2hdc in next stitch, hdc17 (19 sts).
Rnd 21: 2hdc in next stitch, hdc18 (20 sts).
Rnd 22: 2hdc in next stitch, hdc19 (21 sts).
Rnd 23: 2hdc in next stitch, hdc20 (22 sts).
Rnd 24: 2hdc in next stitch, hdc21 (23 sts).
Rnd 25: 2hdc in next stitch, hdc22 (24 sts).
Rnd 26: 2hdc in next stitch, hdc23 (25 sts).
Rnd 27: 2hdc in next stitch, hdc24 (26 sts).
Rnd 28–35: Hdc26.
Rnd 36: Hdc26, sl st to first stitch of rnd to join.
Rows 37–46: Turn, ch2, hdc18 (20 sts).
Fasten off.
Turn work wrong side out. With yarn needle, sew heel together.

Cuff
Turn work right side out.
Rnd 1: Using Color A, join yarn at seam, using ends of rows as stitches, ch2, hdc26, sl st to first stitch to join (26 sts).
Rnds 2–5: Working continuously in the round, ch2, hdc26.
Row 4: Turn, ch2, through back loop only, hdc26, do not join.
Rows 5–8: Turn, ch2, hdc26.
Row 9: Fasten off Color A, join Color B, ch1, sl st in each stitch.
Row 10: Ch3, sl st to same stitch, *sl st to next stitch, ch3, sl st to same stitch, repeat from * to complete row.
Fasten off. Weave in ends.

Skill Level: Beginner

Simply Divine Moccasins

These slippers are super easy and fast to crochet!

Finished Measurements
Women's Small: 8"/20.5 cm long, 3.5"/ 8.9 cm wide
Women's Medium: 9"/23 cm long, 4"/ 10 cm wide
Women's Large: 10"/25.5 cm long, 4"/10cm wide

Yarn
- Yarn Bee Ashley, medium worsted weight #4 yarn, 56% wool/44% polyester (134 yd/123 m, 4 oz/113 g per skein)
  1 skein #20 Cafe

Hook and Other Materials
- US H-8/5.0 mm crochet hook or size to obtain gauge
- Yarn needle

Gauge
7 sts and 8 rows in dc = 4"/10 cm square

Notes
- The slippers are worked from toe to heel, first in joined rounds, then in rows to create the opening for the foot.

Small (make 2)
Ch4.
Rnd 1: 16dc in first chain, sl st to first dc to join rnd (16 sts).
Rnd 2: Ch2 (does not count as a stitch here and throughout), *dc, 2dc in next stitch, repeat from * to complete rnd, sl st to first stitch to join (24 sts).
Rnds 3–7: Ch2, dc in each stitch, sl st to first stitch to join rnd.
Row 8: Ch2, dc16 (16 sts).
Rows 9–15: Turn, ch2, dc16.
Fasten off, leaving a long tail.

Medium (make 2)
Ch4.
Rnd 1: 16dc in first chain, sl st to first dc to join rnd (16 sts).
Rnd 2: Ch2 (does not count as a stitch here and throughout), *dc, 2dc in next stitch, repeat from * to complete rnd, sl st to first stitch to join (24 sts).
Rnds 3–7: Ch2, dc in each stitch, sl st to first stitch to join rnd.
Row 8: Ch2, dc16 (16 sts).
Rows 9–17: Turn, ch2, dc16.
Fasten off, leaving a long tail.

Large (make 2)
Ch4.
Rnd 1: 16dc in first chain, sl st to first dc to join rnd (18 sts).
Rnd 2: Ch2 (does not count as a stitch here and throughout), *dc, 2dc in next stitch, repeat from * to complete rnd, sl st to first stitch to join (27 sts).
Rnds 3–7: Ch2, dc in each stitch, sl st to first stitch to join rnd.
Row 8: Ch2, dc18 (18 sts).
Rows 9–19: Turn, ch2, dc18.
Fasten off, leaving a long tail.

Finishing for All Sizes
With wrong sides facing, fold the back of the slipper in half so that the first stitch of the last row matches up with the final stitch. Using yarn needle, sew heel together. Fasten off.
Join yarn at top of seam for heel, ch1, using ends of rows as stitches, 2sc in each dc row end around foot opening, sl st to first stitch to join rnd.
Fasten off. Weave in all ends.

Skill Level: Intermediate

Double-Strap Slip-Ons

70

Every woman deserves a touch of luxury, and these shoes are just that. Slip them on and relax knowing you're wearing not only the most comfortable slippers, but the cutest too!

Finished Measurements
Women's Small: 8"/20.5 cm long, 3.5"/8.9 cm wide
Women's Medium: 9"/23 cm long, 4"/10 cm wide
Women's Large: 10"/25.5 cm long, 4"/10 cm wide

Yarn
- Lion Brand Tweed Stripes, bulky weight #5 yarn, 100% acrylic (144 yd/132 m, 3 oz/85 g per skein) 2 skeins #753-203 Tundra

Hook and Other Materials
- US F-5/3.75 mm crochet hook or size to obtain gauge
- 2 stitch markers
- 4 medium dark brown buttons
- Yarn needle
- Sewing thread in matching color and needle

Gauge
16 sts and 12 rows in hdc = 4"/10 cm square

Notes
- Each slipper is worked from the center of the sole up in rounds. The heels and straps are crocheted directly onto the finished slipper.
- If you like, mark the first stitch of the round with a stitch marker.
- Do not count the first ch1, ch2 or the last sl st as a stitch.
- For tutorials on Double Crochet Decrease (dc dec), Half Double Crochet Decrease (hdc dec), and Single Crochet Decrease (sc dec), see pages 90, 88, and 87.

Small (make 2)
Ch20.

Rnd 1: Turn, sc in second chain from hook, sc8, hdc9, 6hdc in last chain, working continuously onto opposite side of chain, hdc9, sc9, sl st to first stitch to join rnd (42 sts).

Rnd 2: Ch1, 2sc in same stitch, sc6, hdc7, dc4, 2dc in next 6 stitches, dc4, hdc7, sc6, 2sc in last stitch, sl st to first stitch to join rnd (50 sts).

Rnd 3: Ch1, sc in same stitch, 2sc in next stitch, sc6, hdc7, dc4, *dc, 2dc in next stitch, repeat from * 5 more times, dc4, hdc7, sc6, 2sc in next stitch, sc in last stitch, sl st to first stitch to join rnd (58 sts).

Rnd 4: Ch1, sc in same stitch, sc in next stitch, 2sc in next stitch, sc3, hdc17, *hdc2, 2hdc in next stitch, repeat from * 5 more times, hdc17, sc3, 2sc in next stitch, sc2, sl st to first stitch to join rnd (66 sts).

Rnd 5: Ch1, sc in each stitch, sl st to first stitch to join rnd.

Rnd 6: Ch2, dc in same stitch, dc2, hdc17, dc dec 12 times, hdc17, dc3, sl st to first stitch to join rnd (54 sts).

Rnd 7: Ch2, dc in same stitch, dc2, hdc15, hdc dec 8 times, hdc15, dc3, sl st to first stitch to join rnd (46 sts).

Rnd 8: Ch2, dc in same stitch, dc2, hdc17, hdc dec 6 times, hdc13, dc3, sl st to first stitch to join rnd (40 sts).

Rnd 9: Ch2, dc in same stitch, dc2, hdc9 (mark last hdc with stitch marker), bpsc22, hdc9 (mark first hdc with stitch marker), dc3, sl st to first stitch to join rnd.

Fasten off. Weave in ends.

Medium (make 2)
Ch24.

Rnd 1: Turn, sc in second chain from hook, sc10, hdc11, 6hdc in last chain, working continuously onto opposite side of chain, hdc11, sc11, sl st to first stitch to join rnd (50 sts).

Rnd 2: Ch1, 2sc in same stitch, sc10, hdc7, dc4, 2dc in next 6 stitches, dc4, hdc7, sc10, 2sc in last stitch, sl st to first stitch to join rnd (58 sts).

Rnd 3: Ch1, sc in same stitch, 2sc in next stitch, sc10, hdc7, dc4, *dc, 2dc in next stitch, repeat from * 5 more times, dc4, hdc7, sc10, 2sc next stitch, sc in last stitch, sl st to first stitch to join rnd (64 sts).

Rnd 4: Ch1, sc in same stitch, sc in next stitch, 2sc in next stitch, sc3, hdc18, *hdc2, 2hdc in next stitch, repeat from * 5 more times, hdc18, sc3, 2sc in next stitch, sc2, sl st to first stitch to join rnd (72 sts).

Rnd 5: Ch1, sc in each stitch, sl st to first stitch to join rnd.

Rnd 6: Ch2, dc in same stitch, dc2, hdc21, dc dec 12 times, hdc21, dc3, sl st to first stitch to join rnd (60 sts).

Rnd 7: Ch2, dc in same stitch, dc2, hdc19, hdc dec 8 times, hdc19, dc3, sl st to first stitch to join rnd (52 sts).

Rnd 8: Ch2, dc in same stitch, dc2, hdc17, hdc dec 6 times, hdc17, dc3, sl st to first stitch to join rnd (46 sts).

Rnd 9: Ch2, dc in same stitch, dc2, hdc9 (mark last hdc with stitch marker), bpsc28, hdc9 (mark first hdc with stitch marker), dc3, sl st to first stitch to join rnd.

Fasten off. Weave in ends.

Large (make 2)
Ch28.

Rnd 1: Turn, sc in second chain from hook, sc12, hdc13, 6hdc in last chain, working continuously onto opposite side of chain, hdc13, sc13, sl st to first stitch to join rnd (58 sts).

Rnd 2: Ch1, 2sc in same stitch, sc10, hdc10, dc5, 2dc in next 6 stitches, dc5, hdc10, sc10, 2sc in last stitch, sl st to first stitch to join rnd (66 sts).

Rnd 3: Ch1, sc in same stitch, 2sc in next stitch, sc10, hdc10, dc5, *dc, 2dc in next stitch, repeat from * 5 more times, dc5, hdc10, sc10, 2sc next stitch, sc in last stitch, sl st to first stitch to join rnd (74 sts).

Rnd 4: Ch1, sc in same stitch, sc in next stitch, 2sc in next stitch, sc3, hdc22, *hdc2, 2hdc in next stitch, repeat from * 5 more times, hdc22, sc3, 2sc in next stitch, sc2, sl st to first stitch to join rnd (82 sts).

Rnd 5: Ch1, sc in each stitch, sl st to first stitch to join rnd.

Rnd 6: Ch2, dc in same stitch, dc2, hdc26, dc dec 12 times, hdc26, dc3, sl st to first stitch to join rnd (70 sts).

Rnd 7: Ch2, dc in same stitch, dc2, hdc24, hdc dec 8 times, hdc24, dc3, sl st to first stitch to join rnd (62 sts).

Rnd 8: Ch2, dc in same stitch, dc2, hdc22, hdc dec 6 times, hdc22, dc3, sl st to first stitch to join rnd (56 sts).

Rnd 9: Ch2, dc in same stitch, dc2, hdc9 (mark last hdc with stitch marker), bpsc34, hdc9 (mark first hdc with stitch marker), dc3, sl st to first stitch to join rnd.

Fasten off. Weave in ends.

Cuff Straps for All Sizes
Right Slipper: Join yarn on right side of shoe at stitch marker; **Left Slipper:** Join yarn on left side of shoe at stitch marker.

Row 1: Ch2, dc in same stitch, dc23 (24 sts).

Row 2: Turn, ch2, dc in same stitch, dc dec 2 times, dc16, dc dec 2 times, dc in last stitch (last stitch will be between the ch2 and dc on previous row to create a smooth finish here and throughout) (20 sts).

Row 3: Turn, ch2, dc in same stitch, dc dec, dc14, dc dec, dc in last stitch, ch25 (first strap) (43 sts).

Row 4: Turn, dc in third stitch from hook, dc in each chain and stitch across row (42 sts).

Row 5: Turn, ch2, dc in same stitch, dc 17, ch25 (second strap) (43 sts).

Row 6: Turn, dc in third stitch from hook, dc in each chain and stitch across row (42 sts).

Fasten off. Weave in ends.

Using sewing needle and thread, sew buttons onto opposite sides of straps. Push buttons through dc stitches to finish.

Skill Level: Intermediate

Miss Kitty Slippers

*E*very woman with a cat understands that these slippers are a necessity! Slip them on and snuggle up with this cute pair of kitties.

Finished Measurements
Women's Small: 8"/20.5 cm long, 3.5"/8.9 cm wide
Women's Medium: 9"/23 cm long, 4"/10 cm wide
Women's Large: 10"/25.5 cm long, 4"/10 cm wide

Yarn
- Lion Brand Vanna's Choice, medium worsted weight #4 yarn, 100% acrylic (170 yd/156 m, 3.5 oz/100 g per skein)
    1 skein #860-153 Black (Color A)
    1 skein #860-101 Pink (Color B)
    1 skein #860-100 White (Color C)
- Lion Brand Fun Fur Yarn, bulky weight #5 yarn, 100% polyester (64 yd/58 m, 1.75 oz/50 g per skein)
    1 skein #320-153 Black (Color D)

Hook and Other Materials
- US H-8/5 mm crochet hook or size to obtain gauge
- 2 stitch markers
- Yarn needle
- 4 small amigurumi animal eyes

Gauge
16 sts and 12 rows in hdc = 4"/10 cm square

Notes
- Each slipper is worked from the center of the sole up.
- If you like, mark the beginning of the round with a stitch marker.
- Do not count the first ch1 or ch2 or the last sl st as a stitch.
- For tutorials on Double Crochet Decrease (dc dec), Half Double Crochet Decrease (hdc dec), and Single Crochet Decrease (sc dec), see pages 90, 88, and 87.

Small (make 2)
Using Color A, ch20.
Rnd 1: Turn, sc in second chain from hook, sc8, hdc9, 6hdc in last chain, working continuously onto opposite side of chain, hdc9, sc9, sl st to first stitch to join rnd (42 sts).
Rnd 2: Ch1, 2sc in same stitch, sc6, hdc7, dc4, 2dc in next 6 stitches, dc4, hdc7, sc6, 2sc in last stitch, sl st to first stitch to join rnd (50 sts).
Rnd 3: Ch1, sc in same stitch, 2sc in next stitch, sc6, hdc7, dc4 *dc, 2dc in next stitch, repeat from * 5 more times, dc4, hdc7, sc6, 2sc next stitch, sc in last stitch, sl st to first stitch to join rnd (58 sts).
Rnd 4: Ch1, sc in same stitch, sc in next stitch, 2sc in next stitch, sc3, hdc17, *hdc2, 2hdc in next stitch, repeat from * 5 more times, hdc17, sc3, 2sc in next stitch, sc2, sl st to first stitch to join rnd (66 sts).
Rnd 5: Join Color D. Holding Color A and D together, ch1, sc in each stitch, sl st to first stitch to join rnd.
Rnd 6: Ch2, dc in same stitch, dc2, hdc17, dc dec 12 times, hdc17, dc3, sl st to first stitch to join rnd (54 sts).
Rnd 7: Ch2, dc in same stitch, dc2, hdc15, hdc dec 8 times, hdc15, dc3, sl st to first stitch to join rnd (46 sts).
Rnd 8: Ch2, dc in same stitch, dc2, hdc17, hdc dec 6 times, hdc13, dc3, sl st to first stitch to join rnd (40 sts).
Rnd 9: Drop Color D. With Color A, ch2, hdc in each stitch, sl st to first stitch to join rnd.
Fasten off A and D. Weave in all ends.

Medium (make 2)
Using Color A, ch24.
Rnd 1: Turn, sc in second chain from hook, sc10, hdc11, 6hdc in last chain, working continuously onto opposite side of chain, hdc11, sc11, sl st to first stitch to join rnd (50 sts).
Rnd 2: Ch1, 2sc in same stitch, sc10, hdc7, dc4, 2dc in next 6 stitches, dc4, hdc7, sc10, 2sc in last stitch, sl st to first stitch to join rnd (58 sts).
Rnd 3: Ch1, sc in same stitch, 2sc in next stitch, sc10, hdc7, dc4 *dc, 2dc in next stitch, repeat from * 5 more times, dc4, hdc7, sc10, 2sc next stitch, sc in last stitch, sl st to first stitch to join rnd (64 sts).
Rnd 4: Ch1, sc in same stitch, sc in next stitch, 2sc in next stitch, sc3, hdc18, *hdc2, 2hdc in next stitch, repeat from * 5 more times, hdc18, sc3, 2sc in next stitch, sc2, sl st to first stitch to join rnd (72 sts).
Rnd 5: Join Color D. Holding Color A and D together, ch1, sc in each stitch, sl st to first stitch to join rnd (72 sts).
Rnd 6: Ch2, dc in same stitch, dc2, hdc21, dc dec 12 times, hdc21, dc3, sl st to first stitch to join rnd (60 sts).
Rnd 7: Ch2, dc in same stitch, dc2, hdc19, hdc dec 8 times, hdc19, dc3, sl st to first stitch to join rnd (52 sts).
Rnd 8: Ch2, dc in same stitch, dc2, hdc17, hdc dec 6 times, hdc17, dc3, sl st to first stitch to join rnd (46 sts).
Rnd 9: Drop Color D. With Color A, ch2, hdc in each stitch, sl st to first stitch to join rnd.
Fasten off A and D. Weave in all ends.

Large (make 2)

Using Color A, ch28.

Rnd 1: Turn, sc in second chain from hook, sc12, hdc13, 6hdc in last chain, working continuously onto opposite side of chain, hdc13, sc13, sl st to first stitch to join rnd (58 sts).

Rnd 2: Ch1, 2sc in same stitch, sc10, hdc10, dc5, 2dc in next 6 stitches, dc5, hdc10, sc10, 2sc in last stitch, sl st to first stitch to join rnd (66 sts).

Rnd 3: Ch1, sc in same stitch, 2sc in next stitch, sc10, hdc10, dc5 *dc, 2dc in next stitch, repeat from * 5 more times, dc5, hdc10, sc10, 2sc next stitch, sc in last stitch, sl st to first stitch to join rnd (74 sts).

Rnd 4: Ch1, sc in same stitch, sc in next stitch, 2sc in next stitch, sc3, hdc22, *hdc2, 2hdc in next stitch, repeat from * 5 more times, hdc22, sc3, 2sc in next stitch, sc2, sl st to first stitch to join rnd (82 sts).

Rnd 5: Join Color D. Holding Color A and D together, ch1, sc in each stitch, sl st to first stitch to join rnd (82 sts).

Rnd 6: Ch2, dc in same stitch, dc2, hdc26, dc dec 12 times, hdc26, dc3, sl st to first stitch to join rnd (70 sts).

Rnd 7: Ch2, dc in same stitch, dc2, hdc24, hdc dec 8 times, hdc24, dc3, sl st to first stitch to join rnd (62 sts).

Rnd 8: Ch2, dc in same stitch, dc2, hdc22, hdc dec 6 times, hdc22, dc3, sl st to first stitch to join rnd (56 sts).

Rnd 9: Drop Color D. With Color A, ch2, hdc in each stitch, sl st to first stitch to join rnd.

Fasten off A and D. Weave in all ends.

Top of Slipper for All Sizes (make 2)

Using Color A, ch9.

Row 1: Turn, sc in second chain from hook and in each across (8 sts).

Rows 2–7: Turn, ch1, sc in each stitch.

Row 8: Turn, sc dec, sc4, sc dec (6 sts).

Row 9: Turn, sc dec, sc2, sc dec (4 sts).

Fasten off, leaving a 10"/25.5 cm tail.

Using yarn needle, start in the middle and working to each side, sew the tops onto each of the slippers.

Ears for All Sizes (make 4)

Using Color B, ch2.

Row 1: Turn, 2sc in first chain (2 sts).

Row 2: Turn, 2sc in each stitch (4 sts).

Rows 3–4: Turn, ch1, sc in each stitch.

Fasten off. Weave in ends.

Join Color A at bottom right corner of ear. Using the ends of rows as stitches, sc up the ear, (sc, ch1, sc) in the top stitch, sc down the ear.

Fasten off, leaving a 10"/25.5 cm tail.

Using yarn needle, sew an ear onto each side of top of slipper.

Finishing for All Sizes

Position the eyes on the slipper and attach them.

Using the yarn needle and Color B, stitch on the nose. Fasten off.

With Color C, stitch on the whiskers. Fasten off.

Weave in all ends.

Skill Level: Beginner

Super Kozy Kidz Slipper Socks

My son claimed these slippers for himself the moment he tried them on, proclaiming, "These are cozy!" If you can keep shoes on a six-year-old kiddo, then you've hit the jackpot! These are perfect for any season, boy or girl, and super easy to crochet. Make them in multiple colors to match their PJs.

Finished Measurements
Children's Small: 7"/18 cm long, 3"/7.75 cm wide
Children's Medium: 8"/20.5 cm long, 3.5"/9 cm wide
Children's Large: 9"/23 cm long, 4"/10 cm wide

Yarn
- Yarn Bee Fleece Lite, bulky weight #5 yarn, 97% acrylic/3% polyester (112 yd/102 m, 5 oz/142 g per skein) 1 skein #52 Seaglass

Hook and Other Materials
- US I-9/5.5 mm crochet hook or size to obtain gauge
- Yarn needle

Gauge
10 sts and 6 rows in dc = 4"/10 cm square

Notes
- Each slipper is worked from the toe to the heel. The first section is worked in the round, then in rows for the heel section. The slipper is finished by working across the top in the round to create a finished edge.
- The ch2 at the beginning of the rounds does not count as a stitch. It is used to create a hidden seam. The ch3 at the beginning of the row counts as a dc.
- For a tutorial on Double Crochet Decrease (dc dec), see page 90.

Small (make 2)
Ch4.
Rnd 1: 7dc in first chain, sl st to first dc to join rnd (7 sts).
Rnd 2: Ch2, 2dc in each stitch, sl st to first stitch to join rnd (14 sts).
Rnds 3–6: Ch2, dc in each stitch, sl st to first stitch to join rnd.
Row 7: Ch3, dc8 (9 sts).
Row 8: Turn, ch3, dc8.
Row 9: Turn, ch3, dc, dc dec, dc, dc dec, dc2 (7 sts).
Rnd 10: Sl st to opposite corner to join heel, ch1, using the edges of the rows as stitches, 2sc in end of each dc row (4 sts), sl st across top of foot (5 sts), 2sc in end of each dc row (4 sts), sl st to first stitch to join (13 sts).
Fasten off, leaving a long tail. Using yarn needle, sew heel together. Weave in ends.

Medium (make 2)
Ch4.
Rnd 1: 8dc in first chain, sl st to first dc to join rnd (8 sts).
Rnd 2: Ch2, 2dc in each stitch, sl st to first stitch to join rnd (16 sts).
Rnds 3–7: Ch2, dc in each stitch, sl st to first stitch to join rnd.
Row 8: Ch3, dc10 (11 sts).
Rows 9–10: Turn, ch3, dc10.
Row 10: Turn, ch3, dc2, dc dec, dc, dc dec, dc3 (9 sts).
Rnd 11: Sl st to opposite corner to join heel, ch1, using the edges of the rows as stitches, 2sc in end of each dc row (6 sts), sl st across top of foot (5 sts), 2sc in end of each dc row (6 sts), sl st to first stitch to join (17 sts).
Fasten off, leaving a long tail. Using yarn needle, sew heel together. Weave in ends.

Large (make 2)
Ch4.
Rnd 1: 9dc in first chain, sl st to first dc to join rnd (9 sts).
Rnd 2: Ch2, 2dc in each stitch, sl st to first stitch to join rnd (18 sts).
Rnds 3–8: Ch2, dc in each stitch, sl st to first stitch to join rnd.
Row 9: Ch3, dc11 (12 sts).
Rows 10–11: Turn, ch3, dc11.
Row 12: Turn, ch3, dc2, dc dec 3 times, dc3 (9 sts).
Rnd 13: Sl st to opposite corner to join heel, ch1, using the edges of the rows as stitches, 2sc in end of each dc row (6 sts), sl st across top of foot (6 sts), 2sc in end of each dc row (6 sts), sl st to first stitch to join (18 sts).
Fasten off, leaving a long tail. Using yarn needle, sew heel together. Weave in ends.

Skill Level: Intermediate

Twilight Boots

Keep warm in style with this slipper-leg warmer mash-up.

Finished Sole Measurements
Women's Small: 5"/12.75 cm long
Women's Medium: 6"/15.25 cm long
Women's Large: 7"/17.75 cm long

Yarn
- Red Heart Midnight Boutique, medium worsted weight #4 yarn, 65% acrylic/23%wool/6% metallic polyester (153 yd/140 m, 7 oz/2.5 g per skein)
  2 skeins #1945 Shadow

Hook and Other Materials
- US H-8/5 mm crochet hook or size to obtain gauge
- Yarn needle

Gauge
14 sts and 14 rows in sc = 4"/10 cm square

Notes
- The boot is made in a single panel from leg to toe, and then sewn together to finish.
- For tutorials on Single Crochet Decrease (sc dec) and Treble Crochet (tr), see pages 87 and 96.

Small (make 2)
Ch28.
Row 1: Turn, sc in second chain from hook and in each across (27 sts).
Row 2: Turn, ch2, hdc in each stitch.
Row 3: Turn, ch1, sc in each stitch.
Rows 4–10: Repeat Rows 2 and 3, ending on Row 2.
Row 11: Turn, sc dec, sc23, sc dec (25 sts).
Rows 12–18: Repeat Rows 2 and 3, ending on Row 2.
Row 19: Turn, ch1, sc11, 2sc in next stitch, ch1, skip 1 stitch, 2sc in next stitch, sc11 (27 sts).
Row 20: Turn, ch2, hdc13, 7tr in ch1 space, sc13 (33 sts).
Row 21: Turn, ch1, sc15, 2sc in next stitch, ch1, skip 1 stitch, 2sc in next stitch, sc15 (35 sts).
Row 22: Turn, ch2, hdc17, 7tr in ch1 space, hdc17 (41 sts).
Row 23: Turn, ch1, sc19, 2sc in next stitch, ch1, skip 1 stitch, 2sc in next stitch, sc19 (43 sts).
Row 24: Turn, ch2, hdc21, 7tr in ch1 space, hdc21 (49 sts).
Row 25: Turn, ch1, sc23, 2sc in next stitch, ch1, skip 1 stitch, 2sc in next stitch, sc23 (51 sts).
Row 26: Turn, ch2, hdc25, 7tr in ch1 space, hdc25 (57 sts).
Row 27: Turn, ch1, sc27, 2sc in next stitch, ch1, skip 1 stitch, 2sc in next stitch, sc27 (59 sts).
Row 28: Turn, ch2, hdc29, 7tr in ch1 space, hdc29 (65 sts).
Rows 29–33: Turn, ch1, sc in each stitch.
Row 34: Turn, sc dec, sc61, sc dec (63 sts).
Fasten off. Weave in ends.

Medium (make 2)
Ch30.
Row 1: Turn, sc in second chain from hook and in each across (29 sts).
Row 2: Turn, ch2, hdc in each stitch.
Row 3: Turn, ch1, sc in each stitch.
Rows 4–12: Repeat Rows 2 and 3, ending on Row 2.
Row 13: Turn, sc dec, sc25, sc dec (27 sts).
Rows 14–20: Repeat Rows 2 and 3, ending on Row 2.
Row 21: Turn, ch1, sc12, 2sc in next stitch, ch1, skip 1 stitch, 2sc in next stitch, sc12 (29 sts).
Row 22: Turn, ch2, hdc14, 7tr in ch1 space, sc14 (35 sts).
Row 23: Turn, ch1, sc16, 2sc in next stitch, ch1, skip 1 stitch, 2sc in next stitch, sc16 (37 sts).
Row 24: Turn, ch2, hdc18, 7tr in ch1 space, hdc18 (43 sts).
Row 25: Turn, ch1, sc20, 2sc in next stitch, ch1, skip 1 stitch, 2sc in next stitch, sc20 (45 sts).
Row 26: Turn, ch2, hdc22, 7tr in ch1 space, hdc22 (51 sts).
Row 27: Turn, ch1, sc24, 2sc in next stitch, ch1, skip1 stitch, 2sc in next stitch, sc24 (53 sts).
Row 28: Turn, ch2, hdc26, 7tr in ch1 space, hdc26 (59 sts).
Row 29: Turn, ch1, sc28, 2sc in next stitch, ch1, skip 1 stitch, 2sc in next stitch, sc28 (61 sts).
Row 30: Turn, ch2, hdc30, 7tr in ch1 space, hdc30 (67 sts).
Rows 31–35: Turn, ch1, sc in each stitch.
Row 36: Turn, sc dec, sc63, sc dec (65 sts).
Fasten off. Weave in ends.

Large (make 2)
Ch32.
Row 1: Turn, sc in second chain from hook and in each across (31 sts).
Row 2: Turn, ch2, hdc in each stitch.
Row 3: Turn, ch1, sc in each stitch.
Rows 4–14: Repeat Rows 2 and 3, ending on Row 2.
Row 15: Turn, sc dec, sc27, sc dec (29 sts).
Rows 16–23: Repeat Rows 2 and 3.
Row 24: Turn, ch1, sc13, 2sc in next stitch, ch1, skip 1 stitch, 2sc in next stitch, sc13 (31 sts).
Row 25: Turn, ch2, hdc15, 7tr in ch1 space, sc15 (37 sts).
Row 26: Turn, ch1, sc17, 2sc in next stitch, ch1, skip 1 stitch, 2sc in next stitch, sc17 (39 sts).
Row 27: Turn, ch2, hdc19, 7tr in ch1 space, hdc19 (45 sts).
Row 28: Turn, ch1, sc21, 2sc in next stitch, ch1, skip 1 stitch, 2sc in next stitch, sc21 (47 sts).
Row 29: Turn, ch2, hdc23, 7tr in ch1 space, hdc23 (53 sts).
Row 30: Turn, ch1, sc25, 2sc in next stitch, ch1, skip 1 stitch, 2sc in next stitch, sc25 (55 sts).
Row 31: Turn, ch2, hdc27, 7tr in ch1 space, hdc27 (61 sts).
Row 32: Turn, ch1, sc29, 2sc in next stitch, ch1, skip 1 stitch, 2sc in next stitch, sc29 (63 sts).
Row 33: Turn, ch2, hdc31, 7tr in ch1 space, hdc31 (69 sts).
Rows 34–39: Turn, ch1, sc in each stitch.
Row 40: Turn, sc dec, sc65, sc dec (67 sts).
Fasten off. Weave in ends.

Finishing for All Sizes
Fold the piece in half lengthwise, wrong sides facing out. Leaving the top open, sew together with yarn needle, ending with the toe.
Fasten off. Weave in ends.

How to Read My Patterns

Skill Level

To help you pick a pattern that is consistent with your crochet experience, every pattern in the book indicates its skill level: beginner, intermediate, or advanced. For patterns designated for beginners, you'll need to know how to chain, single crochet, half double crochet, and/or double crochet. As you move up the skill level ladder, more stitch knowledge is required, but there are photo tutorials included in this book for every single stitch you'll need to know. And none of the patterns are difficult. My design goal is always to create the sweetest items using the simplest stitches possible.

Yarn

Under Yarn, you will find listed the specific yarn(s) and colors I used to crochet the pattern, plus how many skeins you'll need. Also included is that specific yarn's "yarn weight." You'll find this information on the label of every skein of yarn you buy, and it ranges from #0 lace weight to #7 jumbo. If you can't find the specific yarn I use or you'd like to use something else, knowing the yarn weight will let you pick another yarn that will have the same gauge.

Standard Yarn Weight System

Categories of yarn, gauge ranges, and recommended needle and hook sizes

Yarn Weight Symbol & Category Names	0 LACE	1 SUPER FINE	2 FINE	3 LIGHT	4 MEDIUM	5 BULKY	6 SUPER BULKY	7 JUMBO
Type of Yarns in Category	Fingering 10-count crochet thread	Sock, Fingering, Baby	Sport, Baby	DK, Light Worsted	Worsted, Afghan, Aran	Chunky, Craft, Rug	Bulky, Roving	Jumbo, Roving
Knit Gauge Range* in Stockinette Stitch to 4 inches	33–40** sts	27–32 sts	23–26 sts	21–24 st	16–20 sts	12–15 sts	6–11 sts	6 sts and fewer
Recommended Needle in Metric Size Range	1.5–2.25 mm	2.25–3.25 mm	3.25–3.75 mm	3.75–4.5 mm	4.5–5.5 mm	5.5–8 mm	8 mm and larger	12.75 mm and larger
Recommended Needle U.S. Size Range	000–1	1 to 3	3 to 5	5 to 7	7 to 9	9 to 11	11 and larger	17 and larger
Crochet Gauge* Ranges in Single Crochet to 4 inch	32–42 double crochets**	21–32 sts	16–20 sts	12–17 sts	11–14 sts	8–11 sts	5–9 sts	6 sts and fewer
Recommended Hook in Metric Size Range	Steel*** 1.6–1.4 mm	2.25–3.5 mm	3.5–4.5 mm	4.5–5.5 mm	5.5–6.5 mm	6.5–9 mm	9 mm and larger	15 mm and larger
Recommended Hook U.S. Size Range	Steel*** 6, 7, 8 Regular hook B–1	B–1 to E–4	E–4 to 7	7 to I–9	I–9 to K–10 1/2	K–10 1/2 to M–13	M–13 and larger	Q and larger

*GUIDELINES ONLY: The above reflect the most commonly used gauges and needle or hook sizes for specific yarn categories.

**Lace weight yarns are usually knitted or crocheted on larger needles and hooks to create lacy, openwork patterns. Accordingly, a gauge range is difficult to determine. Always follow the gauge stated in your pattern.

***Steel crochet hooks are sized differently from regular hooks—the higher the number, the smaller the hook, which is the reverse of regular hook sizing.

Source: Craft Yarn Council of America's www.YarnStandards.com

Sizing

With just a few exceptions, each pattern in this book, whether it is meant for children, women, or men, includes three sizes: Small, Medium, and Large. To determine which size is best for you or whomever you are crocheting for, please refer to the final measurements for each size in the pattern and let them be your guide.

Also, it's very important for you to check your gauge before beginning. Doing so will ensure that your slippers end up achieving the measurements indicated in the pattern.

Hooks and Other Materials

Here you'll find the hook sizes you'll need, plus any additional materials or tools, which most commonly will include stitch markers, a yarn needle, and a sewing needle and thread.

Gauge

The key to crocheting a garment that fits is to check gauge. Every pattern in this book tells you the gauge for that project, namely how many stitches and rows per inch the final measurements (and final fit) were based on.

To check gauge, you need to crochet a sample swatch using the yarn, hook size, and crochet stitch called for. Crochet the swatch at least 1"/2.5 cm larger than required so that you can check the stitches and rows within the swatch to ensure proper gauge. For instance, if the gauge is determined to be 3"/7.6 cm square in single crochet, you will work up a swatch in single crochet at least 4"/10 cm square. Lay a measuring tape on the swatch and count across how many stitches you have in 3"/7.6 cm. Now reposition the tape and measure up and down how many rows you have in 3"/7.6 cm.

If you have more stitches and rows than you should, try the next larger hook size, and make another gauge swatch. Keep doing this until the swatch matches the pattern gauge. If you have fewer stitches and rows than you should, retest your gauge with the next size smaller hook in same way.

Notes

Be sure to read the Notes section before beginning a project. You'll find helpful hints there, including what stitches beyond the basic single crochet and double crochet might be used and cross references to tutorials for them.

Directions

- When a number is before the command, such as 3hdc, you will work in the *same* stitch.
- When a number is after the command, such as hdc3, you will work that command in that number of following stitches.
- The number in parentheses at the end of a round or row is the total number of stitches for that round or row.
- The asterisks will mark a specific placement in a pattern that will be used when repeating sections.
- Working "in the round" means that you will be working in one direction throughout, not back and forth in rows. To work "continuously in the round" means that the rounds will be crocheted without joining.
- When you see commands written within a set of parentheses, all those commands will be crocheted in the same stitch, for example "(ch1, dc, ch1) in the next stitch."

Abbreviations

blo	back loop only
bpdc	back post double crochet
bpsc	back post single crochet
bptr	back post treble crochet
ch	chain
dc	double crochet
dc dec	double crochet decrease
dc 3 tog	double crochet 3 together
dec	decrease
dtr	double treble crochet
flo	front loop only
fpdc	front post double crochet
fpdc dec	front post double crochet decrease
fpsc	front post single crochet
fptr	front post treble crochet
hdc	half double crochet
hdc dec	half double crochet decrease
inc	increase
rev sc	reverse single crochet
sc	single crochet
sc dec	single crochet decrease
sk	skip
sl st	slip stitch
sl st dec	slip stitch decrease
st(s)	stitch(es)
tr	treble crochet

Stitch Guide

Here you will find everything you need to know to crochet the patterns in this book, even if you've never picked up a crochet hook before.

How to Hold a Crochet Hook

There are two ways to hold a hook; use the one that's most comfortable for you.

Over the Hook Hold

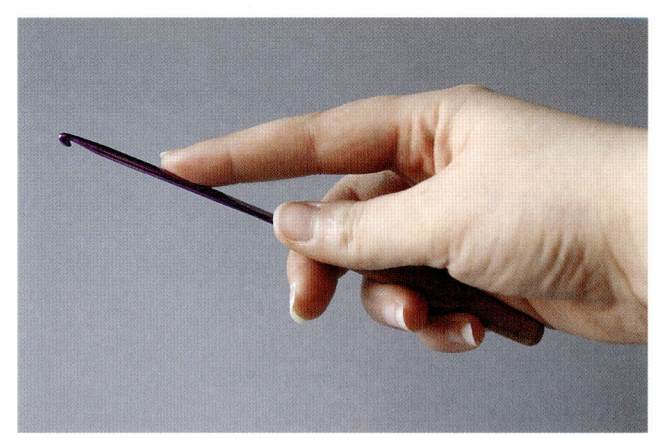

Place your hand over the hook with the handle resting against the palm and your thumb and index finger on the thumb rest.

Under the Hook Hold

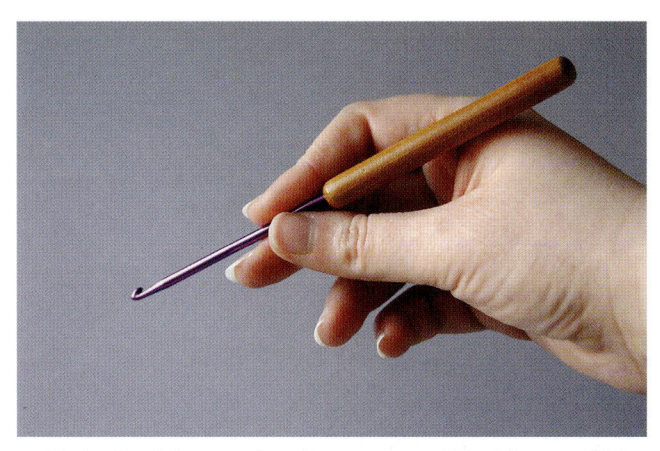

Hold the hook in your hand as you would hold a pencil between your thumb and forefinger.

How to Hold Yarn

Like holding the hook, there are several different ways to hold the yarn when crocheting. Choose the one that is most comfortable. Pay attention to tension, which is how tightly you are pulling on the yarn. You want to maintain an even tension, which will yield a fabric with evenly sized stitches, not too loose and not too tight.

Over the Pinkie Hold

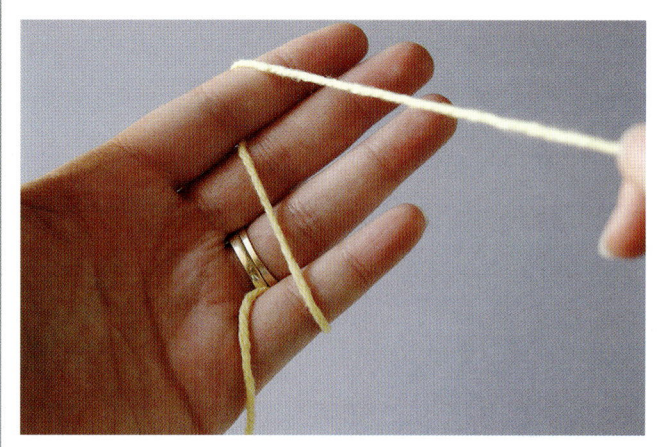

Wrap the yarn over the hand and around your pinky.

Over the Middle Finger Hold

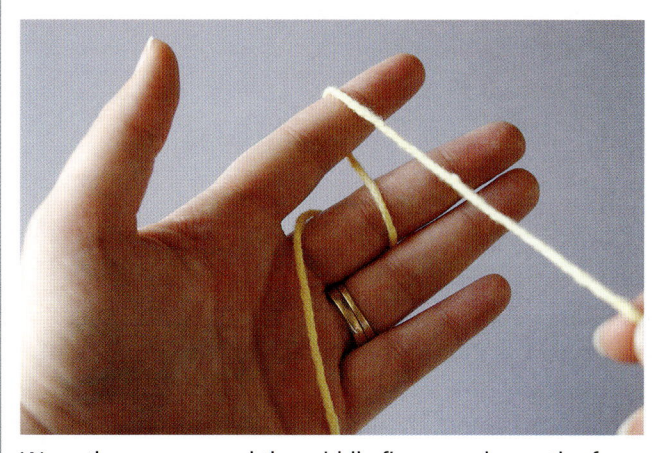

Wrap the yarn around the middle finger and over the forefinger to guide the yarn.

Over the Forefinger Hold

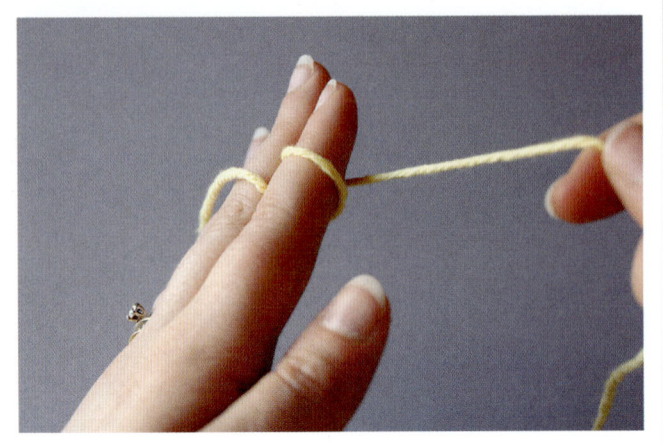

Wrap the yarn around the forefinger.

Slip Knot

This adjustable knot will begin every crochet project.

1. Make a loop in the yarn.

2. With your crochet hook or finger, grab the yarn from the skein and pull through the loop.

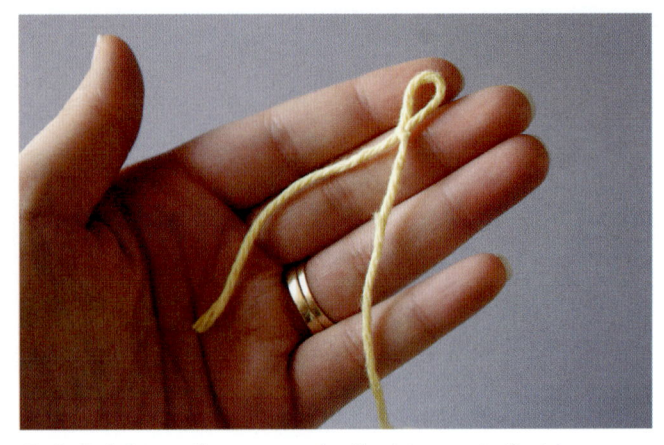

3. Pull tight on the yarn and adjust to create first loop.

Chain (ch)

The chain provides the foundation for your stitches at the beginning of a pattern. It can also serve as a stitch within a pattern and can be used to create an open effect.

1. Insert the hook through the slip knot and yarn over the hook by passing the hook in front of the yarn.

2. Keeping the yarn taut (but not too tight; see Tip below), pull the hook back through the loop with the yarn. Chain 1 is complete.

STITCH GUIDE 85

3. Repeat Steps 1 and 2 to create multiple chains.

Tip: Keep chains loose and not tight to ensure consistency and ease of use.

Anatomy of a Stitch

FRONT LOOP OF STITCH
BACK LOOP OF STITCH

POST

Crocheting into a Stitch

Unless specified otherwise, you will insert your hook under both loops to crochet any stitch.

Crocheting into the Front or Back of a Stitch

At times you will be instructed to work into the front loop only (flo) or the back loop only (blo) of a stitch to create a texture within the pattern.

Inserting hook to crochet into front loop only (flo) of a stitch.

Inserting hook to crochet into back loop only (blo) of a stitch.

Slip Stitch (sl st)

The slip stitch is used to join one stitch to another or to join a stitch to another point.

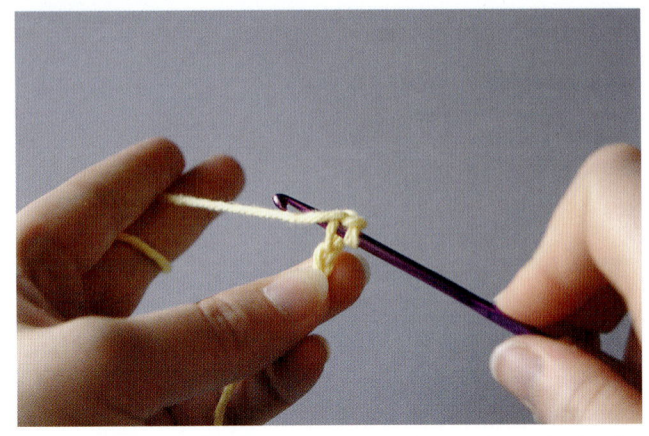

1. Insert the hook from the front of the stitch to the back of stitch and yarn over, just as for a chain stitch.

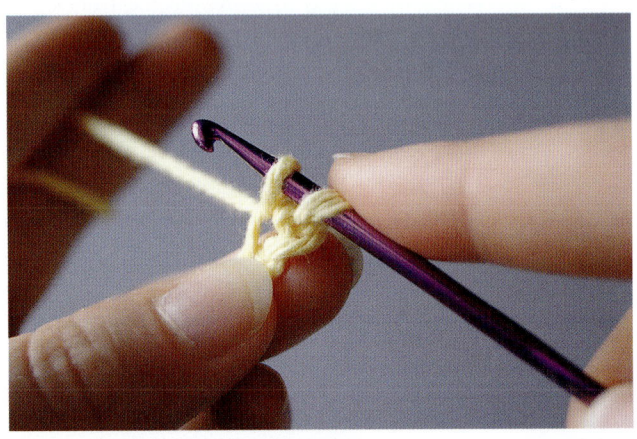

2. Pull the yarn back through the stitch: 2 loops on hook.

3. Continue to pull the loop through the first loop on the hook to finish.

Single Crochet (sc)

1. Insert the hook from the front of the stitch to the back and yarn over.

2. Pull the yarn back through the stitch: 2 loops on hook.

3. Yarn over and draw through both loops on the hook to complete.

Single Crochet Decrease (sc dec)

1. Insert the hook from the front of the stitch to the back and yarn over.

2. Pull the yarn back through the stitch: 2 loops on hook.

3. Leaving the loops on the hook, insert the hook front to back into the next stitch. Yarn over and pull back through stitch: 3 loops on hook.

4. Yarn over and draw through all 3 loops on the hook to complete.

88 STITCH GUIDE

Half Double Crochet (hdc)

1. Yarn over and insert the hook from the front of the stitch to the back.

2. Yarn over and pull yarn back through stitch: 3 loops on hook.

3. Yarn over and draw through all 3 loops on hook to complete.

Half Double Crochet Decrease (hdc dec)

1. Yarn over and insert the hook from the front of the stitch to the back.

2. Yarn over and pull yarn back through stitch: 3 loops on hook.

3. Yarn over and insert hook front to back into the next stitch.

STITCH GUIDE **89**

4. Yarn over and pull yarn back through stitch: 5 loops on hook.

5. Yarn over and pull yarn through all 5 loops on hook to complete.

Double Crochet (dc)

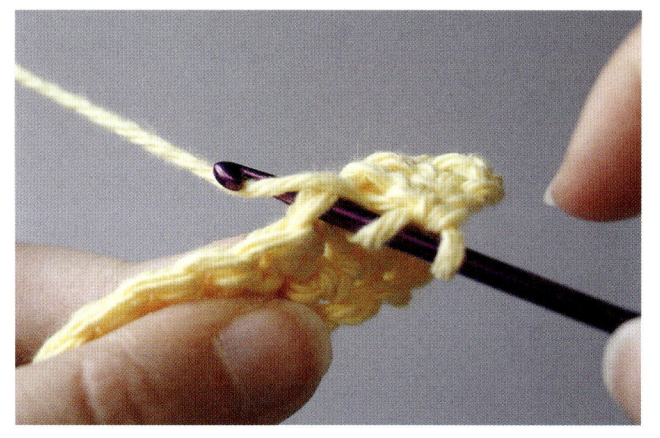

1. Yarn over and insert the hook from the front of the stitch to the back.

2. Yarn over and pull the yarn back through the stitch: 3 loops on hook.

3. Yarn over and draw the yarn through the first 2 loops on the hook: 2 loops on hook.

(continued)

4. Yarn over and draw the yarn through the last 2 loops on hook to complete.

Double Crochet Decrease (dc dec)

1. Yarn over and insert the hook from the front of the stitch to the back.

2. Yarn over and pull the yarn back through the stitch: 3 loops on hook.

3. Yarn over and pull the yarn through the first 2 loops on the hook: 2 loops on hook.

STITCH GUIDE 91

4. Leaving the loops on the hook, insert the hook front to back into the next stitch.

5. Yarn over and pull back through the stitch: 4 loops on hook.

6. Yarn over and pull the yarn through the first 2 loops on the hook: 3 loops on hook.

7. Yarn over and pull the yarn through all 3 loops on hook to complete—1 stitch decreased.

Double Crochet 3 Together (dc 3 tog)

1. Yarn over and insert the hook from the front of the stitch to the back.

2. Yarn over and pull the yarn back through the stitch: 3 loops on hook.

3. Yarn over and pull the yarn through the first 2 loops on the hook: 2 loops on hook.

4. Leaving the loops on the hook, yarn over, insert the hook front to back into the next stitch.

5. Yarn over and pull the yarn back through: 4 loops on hook.

6. Yarn over and pull the yarn through the first 2 loops on the hook: 3 loops on hook.

STITCH GUIDE 93

7. Leaving the loops on the hook, yarn over, and insert the hook into next stitch.

8. Yarn over and pull the yarn back through: 5 loops on hook.

9. Yarn over and pull the yarn through the first 2 loops on the hook: 4 loops on hook.

10. Yarn over and pull the yarn through all the loops on the hook to complete—2 stitches decreased.

Front Post Double Crochet (fpdc)

1. Yarn over and insert the hook from front to back to front of the stitch around the post (see Anatomy of a Stitch on page 85 for where the post is located).

2. Yarn over and pull the yarn back around the post: 3 loops on hook.

3. Yarn over and draw the yarn through the first 2 loops on the hook: 2 loops on hook.

4. Yarn over and draw the yarn through last 2 loops on hook to complete.

Front Post Double Crochet Decrease (fpdc dec)

1. Yarn over and insert the hook from front to back to front of the stitch around the post (see Anatomy of a Stitch on page 85 for where the post is located).

2. Yarn over and pull the yarn back around the post: 3 loops on hook.

3. Yarn over and pull the yarn through the first 2 loops on the hook: 2 loops on hook.

4. Yarn over and insert the hook front to back to front around the next stitch post.

5. Yarn over and pull the yarn through: 4 loops on hook.

6. Yarn over and pull the yarn through the first 2 loops on the hook: 3 loops on hook.

7. Yarn over and pull the yarn through last 2 loops on the hook to complete—1 stitch decreased.

Back Post Double Crochet (bpdc)

1. Yarn over and insert the hook from the back to the front to the back of the stitch around the post (see Anatomy of a Stitch on page 85 for where the post is located). The photo shows the back of the stitch.

2. Yarn over and pull the yarn back around the post: 3 loops on hook.

3. Yarn over and draw the yarn through the first 2 loops on hook: 2 loops on hook.

4. Yarn over and draw the yarn through last 2 loops on hook to complete.

Treble Crochet (tr)

1. Yarn over 2 times and insert the hook from front to back of the stitch.

2. Yarn over and pull the yarn back through the stitch: 4 loops on hook.

3. Yarn over and draw the yarn through the first 2 loops on the hook: 3 loops on hook.

4. Yarn over and draw the yarn through the next 2 loops on the hook: 2 loops on hook.

5. Yarn over and draw the yarn through the last 2 loops on hook to complete.

Front Post Treble Crochet (fptr)

1. Yarn over 2 times.

2. Insert the hook front to back to front around the stitch post (see Anatomy of a Stitch on page 85 for where the post is located).

3. Yarn over and pull yarn back through: 4 loops on hook.

(continued)

STITCH GUIDE

4. Yarn over and pull yarn through 2 loops: 3 loops on hook.

5. Yarn over and pull yarn through 2 loops: 2 loops on hook.

6. Yarn over and pull through the last 2 loops to complete.

Back Post Treble Crochet (bptr)

1. Yarn over 2 times.

2. Insert the hook back to front to back around the stitch post (see Anatomy of a Stitch on page 85 for where the post is located).

3. Yarn over and pull the yarn through: 4 loops on hook.

STITCH GUIDE 99

4. Yarn over and pull the yarn through the first 2 loops on the hook: 3 loops on hook.

5. Yarn over and pull the yarn through the next 2 loops on the hook: 2 loops on hook.

6. Yarn over and pull through the last 2 loops to complete.

Changing Colors

When switching yarns in a piece, use this technique for a clean color change.

1. Insert the hook through the next stitch and pull the yarn back through the stitch.

2. Yarn over with the *next* color and pull through. The color change is complete. Cut the yarn for the original color.

If you are working a color change for a half double crochet, double crochet, or triple crochet, complete the stitch until the last pull through. Yarn over with the *next* color and pull through to complete the color change.

Carrying Yarn

In patterns where you are switching back and forth between colors multiple times, you may be instructed to drop one yarn and pick up another instead of fastening off the original color. This is called carrying a yarn, and it allows you to simply pick the yarn up later, with no ends to weave in. When you carry a yarn or yarns, it's very important to maintain an even tension when you pick up the carried yarn. If the yarn is carried too tightly, your fabric will pucker; if carried too loosely, the stitches can enlarge.

To carry a color, follows Steps 1 and 2 of Changing Colors. Do not cut the yarn when the color change is complete. Continue with Step 3, below.

3. To change colors again, insert the hook through the next stitch and pull the yarn back through the stitch.

4. Drop the current color, yarn over with the color you are carrying, and pull through.

5. Repeat Steps 3 and 4 to carry.

Finishing Touches

Here we cover everything you need for a beautiful finish to your project, from seams to embellishments.

Fasten Off

When you reach the end of your crochet project, you will need to fasten off the yarn. To fasten off simply means to cut the yarn and secure the end. You will also need to fasten off one color to join another color within a project if you are working with multiple colors of yarn.

To fasten off, cut the yarn, leaving a few inches (unless otherwise instructed), and draw the yarn through the last loop on your hook.

Weave in Ends

1. Use your hook or a yarn needle to weave any cut ends up and down through 3 to 4 stitches. I also add a slip stitch to help secure the ends.

2. After weaving it, trim the end as close to the garment as possible to hide the end.

101

Sewing Stitches

In some of these patterns, you will have to sew components of the slipper together. Here are two stitches I often use, worked in a contrasting stitch so that you can see how it is done.

Basic Sewing Stitch

1. Hold the right sides of the items together and, using your needle, go over and under both sets of stitches. Repeat.

This is what the stitches will look like right sides facing out.

Whipstitch

1. Hold the right sides of the pieces together and go under the first 2 sets of stitches. Do not go over the stitches.

2. Turn the needle and go back under the *next* set of stitches. You will be working around the posts of the stitch.

FINISHING TOUCHES 103

As you whipstitch, notice that you're working around the posts and not over the stitches.

This is what the stitches will look like right sides facing out.

Visual Index

U se this handy visual reference to quickly find the slippers you want to crochet.

Shell-Edged Striped Slippers
page 2

Grace Sandals
page 5

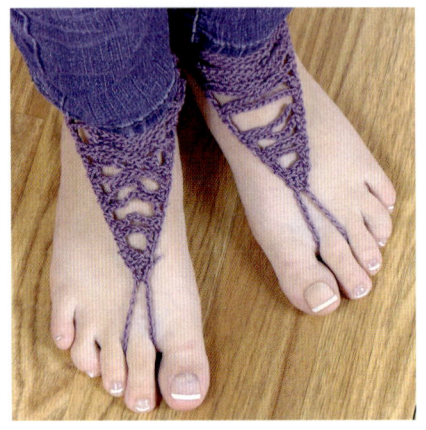

Fun in the Sun Strappy Sandals
page 8

So Comfy Basketweave Socks
page 10

Fuzzy Scuffs
page 13

Rainbow Ruffle Slipper Boots
page 17

Just Peachy Slipper Socks
page 20

VISUAL INDEX 105

Dad Loafers
page 24

**Pearls & Lace
Little Princess Slippers**
page 28

Sandy Button Sandals
page 31

Shaggy Boots
page 36

**Men's Goldenrod
Slipper Socks**
page 39

Frog Loafers
page 42

Cabled Slipper Socks
page 45

Striped Mary Jane Slippers
page 48

**Interlocking Rings
Barefoot Sandals**
page 51

VISUAL INDEX

Ruby Red Slippers
page 54

Fabulous Faux Cable Loafers
page 57

Owl Boots
page 61

Elfin Boot Slippers
page 65

Simply Divine Moccasins
page 68

Double-Strap Slip-Ons
page 70

Miss Kitty Slippers
page 73

Super Kozy Kidz Slipper Socks
page 76

Twilight Boots
page 78